THE
SEX BARRIER
IN
BUSINESS

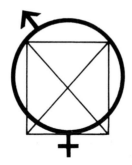

Eleanor Brantley Schwartz

**Publishing Services Division
School of Business Administration
Georgia State University
Atlanta, Georgia**

Published in 1971
Printed in the United States of America
Library of Congress Catalog Card Number: 79-174757
ISBN 0-88406-013-6

Published by:
Publishing Services Division
School of Business Administration
Georgia State University
University Plaza
Atlanta, Georgia, U.S.A 30303

CONTENTS

ACKNOWLEDGMENTS

I am deeply grateful to a number of people for their generous help with this book. It is impossible to acknowledge all fully, but special thanks are due Dr. Francis J. Bridges, Professor of Management, Georgia State University, for his able assistance with the initial structuring of this study, and to the editorial staff of the Bureau of Business and Economic Research (Georgia State University), for their enthusiastic professional guidance.

Finally, I am most appreciative to John III and Cynthia, who patiently understood why this work must be completed.

vi

Chapter I

THE PROBLEM—WOMEN IN MANAGEMENT: CAN THEY BREAK THE BARRIERS?

The position of women in American society is a widely discussed and controversial topic. Certainly, their role is changing. And this change is described, analyzed, diagnosed, and criticized in newspapers, magazines, books, on radio and television, and from the educator's podium. Sociologists, professors, psychologists, anthropologists, philosophers, historians, and other specialists are eager to express their views. Legislation, research, and special programs are concerned with hours, wages, training, and other working arrangements relating to women.

While women are one of the newest challenges to industry, the struggle for "women's rights" has been going on since earliest recorded history. Over the years women have been given property rights and suffrage; they have been admitted to the institutions of higher learning and to the trades and professions. That women work is no longer a subject of major controversy in our society. The question is no longer "Should women work?" but, rather, "At what occupational levels should women work?"

But, as Alan Simpson, the then-new president of Vassar in 1964, commented, "Women have never had it so good and never have they complained so much." Women in the 1970's **are** an uneasy sex.

Changing times have evolved a group of highly motivated, intellectually competent women who want to carry their talents from the home to where the economic activity is. A study of 10,000 Vassar alumnae showed that "most graduates of the mid-50's wanted marriage, with or without a career, while in the mid-60's most were insisting on a career with or without marriage."

Statistical evidence shows, however, that the number of women at the top is infinitesimal. Women rarely rise beyond middle management to the well-paying, prestigious, first-run jobs. Although twenty-nine million women account for over 40 percent of all white-collar jobs, only one out of ten management positions and one out of seven professional jobs are filled by women. While women work in almost every job category listed by the Bureau of the Census, the kind of work that most women do, primarily in low-skill, low-pay jobs, has remained unchanged over the past

1

fifty years. Representation of women in professional and technical job classifications has, in fact, declined from 40 percent in 1950 to 37 percent in 1968. (See Table I.)

Table I

WOMEN IN PROFESSIONAL AND TECHNICAL POSITIONS
1950-1968

| Year | Numbers (in thousands)† | | | Women as Percent of Total |
	Total	Women	Men	
1968*	10,200	3,817	6,382	37.4
1967	9,879	3.697	6,183	37.4
1966	9,310	3,472	5,840	37.3
1965	8,883	3,280	5,602	36.9
1960	7,474	2,706	4,768	36.2
1955	5,792	2,183	3,608	37.7
1950	4,490	1,794	2,696	40.0

SOURCE: Women's Bureau, United States Department of Labor.
†Totals may not add because of rounding.
*Average through September.

Women also earn far less than men. Less than 1 percent of the working women earned $10,000 or more in 1966. The proportion of men earning over $10,000 was almost 20 times higher. The median annual wage for the full-time working man in 1968 was $7,800; for women $4,550.[1] The Administrative Management Society found in a survey that on a national average, men receive $100 to a woman's $60 for the same job. As shown in Chart I, the inequality gap in income between the sexes has grown since World War II.

Legally, individuals, men or women, can no longer be denied jobs, advancement, or equal pay because of sex. In 1964 the Civil Rights Act was passed with "equality for all citizens" as its main objective. Title VII, the provision of the Act which prohibits discrimination in employment based on sex, precludes discrimination with regard to pay and all terms and conditions of employment and union membership.

Nevertheless, it appears barriers against women in other than "traditional" areas of employment (teaching, nursing, clerical) still exist. Despite the increase in women's share of total employment and the rising proportion of women college graduates, very

2

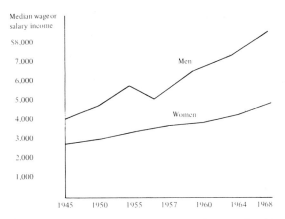

Source: President's Commission Report on the Woman Worker, 1963, p. 56.
Projections to 1968 made on basis of data from *Statistical Abstract*, 1969.

few women are in top management positions. In October 1966, the chairman of the Equal Employment Opportunity Commission released statistics which showed women account for one third to nearly one half of the total white-collar jobs; yet, their representation is very small in "higher echelon managerial jobs." These statistics are from nine Standard Metropolitan Statistical Areas (SMSA's) with populations over 500,000 (Atlanta, Chicago, Cleveland, Kansas City, Los Angeles, New Orleans, New York, San Francisco, and Washington, D. C.) (See Table II for a statistical breakdown of the white-collar work force.)

Ambitious women, in agreement with the conclusion of Harvard Business Review's 1964 study, "the barriers are so great there is scarcely anything to study," complain they are blocked before they begin. While women can obtain the education and experience needed to qualify for top-level executive positions, they feel limited not by their ability or inability but rather by the attitudes of many male executives who still question the ability of women to function successfully in administrative and managerial positions. It is common to hear dedicated working women say they have to be twice as intelligent, three times as industrious, four times as enthusiastic, and work for half the money paid their male counter-

3

Table II

EEO-1 REPORTING SYSTEM: FEMALE EMPLOYMENT STATISTICS, NINE METROPOLITAN AREAS, 1966

Area	Total* White-Collar	Male White-Collar	Female White-Collar	Percent Female of Total White-Collar	White-Collar† Except Clerical	Female White-Collar Except Clerical	Percent Female White-Collar Except Clerical to all White-Collar Except Clerical	Excluding Retail Trade-General Merchandise††		
								White-Collar Except Clerical	Female White-Collar Except Clerical	Percent Female White-Collar Except Clerical to all White-Collar Except Clerical
Atlanta	106,859	56,440	50,419	47.2	58,347	14,650	25.1	46,742	6,479	13.9
Chicago	586,810	325,653	261,157	44.5	326,429	71,113	21.8	279,994	41,771	14.9
Cleveland	157,319	96,555	60,764	38.6	94,747	17,342	18.3	87,857	12,700	14.5
Kansas City	92,038	51,764	40,274	43.8	52,557	12,226	23.3	46,274	7,618	16.5
Los Angeles	528,306	328,691	199,615	37.8	333,654	60,840	18.2	300,080	38,141	12.7
New Orleans	65,242	37,707	27,535	42.2	38,144	8,230	21.6	33,744	5,063	15.0
New York	951,809	519,226	432,583	45.4	492,151	113,063	23.0	437,310	76,409	17.5
San Francisco	219,902	122,932	96,970	44.1	129,150	30,321	23.5	113,575	19,309	17.0
Washington, D.C.	155,735	83,225	72,510	46.6	97,366	27,352	28.1	83,649	18,233	21.8

SOURCE: Office of Research & Reports, Equal Employment Opportunity Commission, Washington, D.C.

*From employers subject to the EEO-1 reporting system. The figures shown are not total employment in areas involved.

†Officials, managers, professionals, technicians, and sales workers.

††Last three columns show "White-Collar Except Clerical" figures which have been adjusted to exclude employment in Retail Trade-General Merchandise, in view of the large number of low-paying sales positions in this industrial classification. They represent, therefore, a more accurate reflection of the distribution of female employees in higher paying white-collar jobs.

4

parts. Even then they may not be taken seriously. Many women feel that no matter how excellent their qualifications, the rise into management is blocked.

Many male executives generally feel men have careers while women have only temporary jobs to tide them over until they find a husband, have the first baby, or pay off the mortgage. These young women, for the most part, are more interested in marriage and drift into and out of employment to suit their temporary needs. Because they make no commitment, employers are less than lukewarm to them. They cannot afford to train women only to lose them. As one senior executive said, "Women just can't cut it in management. At the top, work comes first. Most women aren't willing to put it before her family or friends or pleasure. Besides, we can't depend on them. They come, go, come again, go again. . . ."

But there's a new breed of women, ambitious and dedicated, coming up who are trying to communicate that they are tired of being regarded only as sex symbols. Young women, especially those with college educations, are nonsexual in their outlook. They no longer feel they must be defined just in terms of a relationship to a man—wife, mother, homemaker. They want a career, with or without marriage. The new breed of women feels that ability, not sex, should determine who occupies the executive suite in America's business. Will it?

A shortage of capable talent plagues industry today. As competition grows keener, need for first-rate talent expands even faster. In competition for well-educated, highly motivated executives, will business and service professions turn to their most obvious "natural" resource: Women?

Chapter II

WOMEN'S ROLE: PRE-CIVIL WAR

To appreciate fully the role of women in management in contemporary America, it is helpful to review the social, economic, and leadership responsibilities accorded women in earlier societies. This historical perspective helps provide a background for current attitudes toward women in management. Further, it shows that women have played a wide variety of roles in social organizations. Their emergence from the home and active participation in social, economic, and political affairs is not a phenomenon peculiar to contemporary society. Women have, in fact, been both the "top executives" as well as subordinate in earlier societies. Directly and indirectly, these societies helped influence the modern American view toward utilization of women in decision-making positions. Perhaps the most significant attitudes coloring the outlook were those held toward women in Judaism, the beliefs of the Christian Church regarding the nature of women, and legal developments in England during the eighteenth century.

Ancient Times

Anthropologists, with regard to the part played by women in primitive society, have assigned to women all or the main credit for having effected the first "sharp distinction between the ways of human beings and the ways of beasts of prey."[1]

Creator of civilization. While man hunted, woman developed her talents as homemaker. She learned how to provide clothing for the family, how to make pottery, and other simple household utensils. She began to hoe the land surrounding the primitive homestead, becoming the first agriculturalist.

The peasant stage. The peasant stage of evolution arrived when man entered the economic province of woman, taking over many of her archaic functions. Because women were the first to practice the arts and crafts and husbandry, the custom was deeply embedded that the mothers were the owners of the domestic property and of the fields cultivated by the family. Property passed from mother to daughter. Sons left home to find their brides in other family groups while the daughters, as potential mothers of families, remained in the home.

6

Transition from matriarchy to patriarchy. It commonly is thought that patriarchy has always been the natural state of mankind. Recent research points, however, to an ancient matriarchy when women were looked on as the guiding element in early society. Mystified by her ability to procreate, and enchanted by her domestic science, males believed women were more in touch with the "secret and hidden" forces of nature than they and worshipped her as a goddess. Men were later exalted as gods also, and these gods and goddesses received equal adoration. Only the ancient Hebrews, who finally reduced idolatry when monotheism became their ideal, eliminated the goddesses.

As the transition from matriarchy to patriarchy took place over a long period of time, it was not unusual for matriarchal and patriarchal communities to exist side by side.

Agricultural and pastoral communities. The matriarchal civilizations, self-sufficient and peaceful communities, came into being in fertile valleys with climate favorable for agriculture. Less fertile lands became pastoral communities. In arid lands (Steppes of Asia, for example), the people adopted a nomadic life, and these nomadic women could form no permanent homesteads. The struggle to survive developed aggressive people who descended upon peasant communities, at first destroying them and carrying away the spoils, later settling down and, to some extent, adopting the life style of the conquered people. The warriors' acquisition of wealth became a powerful factor depressing the position of women. This economic power enabled men to transmit their property to their sons; and, as ruler and head of the family, to negotiate the marriage of his children.

Ancient Egypt. The greater part of the ancient matriarchy lies outside written history. Despite anthropological study, knowledge of civilization in far distant antiquity is fragmentary. The most reliable sources are ancient civilizations of Sumeria and Egypt (inscriptions in the temples, tombs), especially as Ancient Egypt preserved a matriarchal way of life into the age of patriarchy, revealing almost unchanged institutions for four thousand years.

Women achieved great importance on the banks of the Nile. Even Pharaoh had to acknowledge his queen, for to her belonged the land of Egypt; the king was the man who married the daughter of his predecessor. Women ruled in Egypt from fourteenth century B. C., and Egypt produced great queens who influenced history.

7

Also, women of Egypt transacted much of the business of the state. They engaged in trade, commerce, banking, law, and agricultural problems. Traditionally, many husbands looked after the home, served as cooks, chambermaids, and nurses.

Sumeria. Historians believe Sumeria's early civilization not dissimilar from Ancient Egypt and that a matriarchal way of life existed. Unlike Egypt, its subsequent course of history was different. Under Hammurabi, Babylonia was unified; and from this earliest known code of law emerged a legal system based on patriarchal ideas. Though woman's position outside the home was generally subordinate, her influence and status were very high within the family. The ancient Jews did not interpret Eve in their myth about the "Fall of Man" as did later literal-minded churchmen during the era of Christianity; they held a high regard and respect for women.

Hebrew legend before Hammurabi's Code include Sarah, Rebecca, Rachel, Leah, Esther the Queen, and Deborah the prophetess, who became ruler of Israel and commander in battle in Eleventh Century B. C. The Song of Deborah is one of the earliest poems.

Influence of Greece. Greek thought provided the main principles from which the social philosophies of the West stemmed—Plato, Aristotle, Pythagoras. Among female Pythagoreans was Pythagoras' wife, Theano, whose fame "for wisdom and virtue was of the highest order." After Pythagoras' death at the end of the sixth or the beginning of the fifth century B. C., Theano carried on the central school of the Order. Plato expressed liberal views about the potentialities of women and argued that "as far as the state is concerned there is no difference between the natures of man and woman." Aristotle, on the other hand, felt men by nature are superior and should rule, while women should be ruled.

Sparta had a liberal view toward women. Women managed the land while men were fighting, and could inherit and retain landed estates as their own. Women were admitted to the gymnasium, and commercial centers appear also to have afforded them educational opportunities.

Athens initially followed matriarchal customs. But as patriarchy asserted itself, it took an unusual form: the Athenian wife never legally entered the household of her husband. She remained under the guardianship of her father, or male next-of-kin, who could, if he wished, take her away from her husband, reclaim her dowry,

8

keep her at home, or marry her to another man. On the death of her husband, however, the wife could make no claim on his property. She returned to her own people.

Rome. In Rome, at the time of the drawing up of The Twelve Tables, a woman passed into the family and power of her husband at marriage. Later, through legal developments the bride remained under the guardianship of her father. As she did not legally become a member of her husband's family, she acquired complete control of her own property. The Roman matron was legally independent with more freedom socially than in any later civilization (until recent times). As Christianity became dominant throughout Europe, women were deprived of this freedom.

The influence of Christianity. Christianity developed as a masculine religion during the time Rome ruled a vast Empire. The Roman matron, through a series of laws, had become emancipated and possessed great freedom. Under Roman law, marriage was a type of partnership between husband and wife, in which the two partners had substantially equal property rights. Her emancipation, however, coincided with the time when great wealth poured into Rome. Citizens became luxury loving and standards declined. The Church felt any latitude accorded women was dangerous and attributed the laxity and decline of the Roman Empire to the emancipation of women.

Early Christian church fathers' vigorous denunciations of Roman women's freedom were an outgrowth of their attitudes toward sex. Sexual activity was carnal; marriage was a concession to the flesh. Thus, a woman was the chief vehicle of sin. Further antifeminism arose from literal interpretations of the "Adam and Eve" myth and the belief that woman caused the "Fall of Man."

The Anglo-Saxon period. Although the Anglo-Saxons were a warlike people honoring male virtues, the position of women was high. A husband never attained such complete power over his wife that she was in a position of subjection. The institution protecting her was her family. One of the chief duties of the family was "avenging wrongs committed to any of its members"; and ill-treatment of a wife could cause a blood feud between two families.

The Middle Ages

A marked characteristic of the Middle Ages, and one which distinguished it from later times, was that women were considered to have great business ability. In an economy that was largely domestic, the industrial center was the home. At its hub stood women. The wife was of tremendous economic importance in the Middle Ages. The man ruled the home; but, nevertheless, there was a sense of partnership existing between husband and wife.

The land was the prime source of economic support from the end of the Roman Empire until the rise of modern commerce and industry. The royal and aristocratic families (the landed families) had heavy obligations connected with the economy of the household and the field. When the baron or knight husband was away in wars, as so often was the case, the woman assumed management responsibilities of the land and the household. She took her husband's place as head of the family, ruled the children, administered estates, collected rents, and, if necessary, acted as attorney in a law suit or organized defense of a manor, and so on. Wives, of necessity, became good businesswomen in addition to their traditional role as mistress of the household.

Whether by apprentice or marriage, women appear to have been admitted into a large number of trades. There were women shipwrights, tailors, spurriers, apothecaries, barbers. Women were also engaged in some of the most remunerative trades and were mercers, drapers, grocers, and merchants.

For centuries, European women displayed great force, directly and indirectly, in the management of state and economy, activities which sustained the monarchy. This was true until the commercial and political revolutions in the eighteenth century disrupted the solidarity of the landed families, and control of the state passed to parliaments.

A well-known French writer, George Francois Renard, said:

It would be a mistake to imagine that the woman of
the Middle Ages was confined to her home, and was
ignorant of the difficulties of a worker's life.
In those days she had an economic independence,
such as is hardly to be met in our time.

The Renaissance
Inherent in Renaissance thought is the conception of woman as fully equal to man and endowed with gifts of mind as well as body. The Renaissance brought a liberation of spirit, awakening women to a sense of intellectual adventure.

The education of women among the higher classes was the same as that of men. Men of the Renaissance accepted this free and easy intellectual and social association with women as a matter of course. There was little question of conscious emancipation,

> ...for the situation was understood to be a matter of course. The education of the women of rank, as well as that of men, sought the development of a well-rounded personality in every respect. The same development of mind and heart that perfected the man was necessary for perfecting woman.[3]

Renaissance ideas never wholly received the sanction of the Church. Nor did such ideas become any more acceptable when the influence of the Reformation swept through Europe. The Reformers had little use for educated women.

Early America

Each major group of American settlers brought a heritage of laws, customs, and religious convictions which largely determined the rights and privileges of their society.

The Dutch, German, Swedish, French groups differed in their beliefs; the Calvinistic Lutherans and Huguenots believed in no rights for married women and developed patriarchal communities. The Pietistic groups believed in complete equality (religious and civil rights) and developed democratic communities.

The English colonies adopted the common law of England which was based on Sir William Blackstone's *Commentaries on the Laws of England*. In the first volume of the *Commentaries,* Blackstone said in his chapter "Of Husband and Wife":

> By marriage, the husband and wife are one person in law; that is, the very being or legal existence of the woman is suspended during the marriage or at least is incorporated and consolidated into that of the husband; under whose wing, protection, and cover, she performs everything; ....Upon this principle of unity of person in husband and wife, depend almost all the legal rights, duties, and disabilities that either of them acquire by the marriage.... A man cannot grant anything to his wife, or enter into covenant with her for the grant would be to suppose her separate existence.... A woman

11

indeed may be attorney for her husband; for that implies no separation from, but is rather a representation of her lord. And a husband may also bequeath any thing to his wife by will; for that cannot take effect till the coverture is determined by his death. The husband is bound to provide his wife with necessaries by law, as much as himself; and if she contracts debts for them, he is obliged to pay them; but for any thing besides necessaries, he is not chargeable. . . . If the wife be indebted before marriage, the husband is bound afterward to pay the debt; for he has adopted her and her circumstances together. . . .

The husband also (by the old law) might give his wife moderate correction. For, as he is to answer for her behavior, the law thought it reasonable to intrust him with this power of restraining her, by domestic chastisement. . . . But, with us, in the politer reign of Charles the second, this power of correction began to be doubted; and a wife may now have security of the peace against her husband; or, in return, a husband against his wife. . . .

These are the chief legal effects of marriage during the covertures; upon which we may observe, that even the disabilities, which the wife lies under, are for the most part intended for her protection and benefit. So great a favorite is the female sex of the laws of England.[4]

By the middle nineteenth century, the *Commentaries* was the prime legal work in the United States and, for nearly a century, a standard textbook for the training of lawyers.

With this legal view in the English colonies, women were *femes soles* if they were spinsters or widows, but they were *femes coverts* if they were married. As *feme coverts,* they had practically no rights; the husband was head of the household, and all that was within was his property, including women.

Blackstone's civil death of married women was a theme of the women's movement at the Seneca Falls, New York, meeting in 1848. In an address to the New York legislature in 1854, Elizabeth Cady Stanton, an outstanding pleader for women's rights, declared that on entering wedlock the woman met "instant civil death." Other women throughout the women's movement also attacked Blackstone's dictum of legal death of women on marriage.

12

Colonial social and economic life. During the Colonial days, women worked in the home, made clothing, and helped their husbands till the soil. Practically all acted as teachers and nurses for their families and for the community, if necessary. When the Westward trek began, women transferred to the covered wagon the tasks they had performed within the home and resumed the same duties when again settled in their new homes.

Around 1820 the American factory system began, and women were a significant part of the labor supply. Lowell, Massachusetts, factory owners began an unusual system of combining work with educational (finishing-school type) courses, which attracted middle-class females. The "Lowell System" continued, successfully, for about fifteen years, when a strike led by the Female Protective Association brought it to a close.

Women did not make much headway in industry until the Civil War, when General Francis E. Spinner, the United States Treasurer, received permission from President Lincoln to hire Jennie Douglas to cut paper currency. From then on, the increase of women in government and industrial work has been continuous. Such things as the development of the typewriter (which opened a new occupation within the white-collar field for women), the adding machine, the telephone, the lightening and simplification of many industrial operations, and the shortages of men resulting from the Civil War helped stimulate employment of women.

Overview

Whether emphasis is placed on records that furnish information about matriarchal societies or patriarchal societies, throughout the ages women have wielded much influence economically, politically, and socially. Women of antiquity initiated or inspired conquests and were intimately involved in political and economic power struggles. For instance, the famed Queen Cleopatra of Egypt, although much remembered for her "sex appeal," was highly educated, a skilled organizer and woman of business. Another queen, Zenobia of Palmyra on the border of the Arabian desert, was also well educated and interested in commerce, politics, and administration. Much political intrigue may be attributed to many ambitious mothers whose political manipulations put their sons in power as emperors, thus influencing and directing the course of political affairs. (For nearly 400 years — until 364 A. D. — the Roman

13

Empire was ruled by men whose mother's maneuvering put them there.) Other powerful women in history include Elizabeth, Queen of England; Marie Antoinette of France; Isabella of Spain; Catherine the Great of Russia; Eleanor of Aquitaine; and Blanche of Castile. Europe was dominated by royal families in which women wielded immense power.

Women of the feudal hierarchy had a status, as did the men; it was a class status, not a status of women as members of a subject sex. Aristocratic women did not view themselves as subjugated. The growth of Christianity in Europe and its doctrine of female inferiority coupled with Blackstone's interpretation of women's rights under English common law curbed women's freedom.

Chapter III

WOMEN'S ROLE: POST-CIVIL WAR

The past one hundred years have witnessed a significant change in the employment of women. In 1890 the Census counted 4 million working women, about one sixth of the work force. About 26.1 million women were in the labor force in April 1965, or one third of the labor force, which compares with 5 million at the turn of the century and with the 1940 prewar figure of slightly less than 14 million.

While many more women now work, both in absolute numbers and as a percent of total female population, than a century ago, there has been little change in the acceptance of women in top management positions. A wide variety of cultural, economic, social, and legal events in the past century have placed an ever-sharpening focus on questions such as, "Are women equal in competency to men in management?" "What should be the role of women in leadership activities?" "Does discrimination against women seeking positions in management, in fact, exist?" "Why do women who now account for one third of the total employment hold only 2 percent of all the top management positions?"

Significant Economic Changes

At the turn of the twentieth century, few socially accepted occupations were open to women. An unmarried woman with no money and no close male relative to support could teach or enter the nursing profession without losing caste. Widows could take in boarders. Women with literary talent could write. The majority of wage-earning women were domestic servants. Usually immigrant women worked in the factories. The principal types of employment, in numerical order, were domestic servant; agricultural laborer; tailoress and seamstress; milliner; dress and mantua maker; teacher; cotton-mill operative; laundress; woolen-mill operative; farmer and planter; and nurse. It was the typewriter that first opened the door to respectable work in business.

Impact of the Industrial Revolution

Perhaps the Industrial Revolution was the most important influence to alter the status of American women. It destroyed the earlier system of home industry which had given women some

15

security. Industrialization resulted in concentration of population near factory sites. This migration from the farm to the city profoundly affected women's work. No longer was she an economically contributing partner in the family's common work. Most farmwomen had worked side-by-side with their husbands as part of a family enterprise; many had run farms on their own. Even among the well-to-do, the ability to carry on household economic activities was an important criterion of a good wife in 1890.

Education for women

Through the devoted work of countless pioneers in the mid-nineteenth century, the doors of secondary and higher education slowly opened to women. Along with the improvement in education came alleviation in the economic position of women. In addition to nursing and teaching, a growing demand arose, through the expansion of commerce, for clerks, shop assistants, telephone operators, and with the invention of the typewriter, stenographers. As education improved, increasing numbers of women entered these occupations.

The general rationale for a daughter's education was that, if the daughter had a useful skill, such as teaching, she could support herself until she found a husband. Or, if she did not marry, or the marriage failed, or her husband became ill and died, she could take care of herself and children.

The suffragette movement

The suffragette movement, which lasted from 1848 to 1920, also helped to break down barriers for women. Suffragettes appealed to legislators and businessmen for legal maximum working hours and, generally, legal status for women in voting and in marriage. The suffragette movement culminated in the 19th amendment, granting women the right to vote.

Impact of wars

During the first World War, women were hired for all kinds of jobs at pay rates never before offered them. This helped destroy the belief that women were incapable of performing jobs previously reserved for men. The men were expected to return home after the war, but many did not. Instead, women claimed better employment conditions and wages.

It was World War II that accelerated long-run changes in the use of women in business. World War I did not lead to heavy reliance on womanpower. The United States was involved in the war only twenty months—long enough to modify traditional patterns of "men's" and "women's" work, but too short to effect permanent changes in women's employment. Under pressure of World War II, when technological changes were demanding more brainpower, many women assumed responsible positions. They accounted for only 25 percent of all workers at the beginning of the war; but by the end of the war in 1945, they represented 36 percent of the total civilian working population. Their participation in the work force continues to increase, as illustrated in Table III.

Table III

WOMEN IN THE LABOR FORCE, SELECTED YEARS, 1890-1965
(14 years of age and over)

Year	Number	As percent of all workers	As percent of woman population
HIGHLIGHTS[1]			
April 1965	26,108,000	35.0	37.3
Start of the sixties			
(April 1960)	23,239,000	33.3	36.3
Midfifties			
(April 1955)	20,154,000	31.2	33.8
Korean conflict			
(April 1953)	19,296,000	30.6	33.1
Pre-Korean conflict			
(April 1950)	18,063,000	29.0	32.1
Post-World War II			
(April 1947)	16,320,000	27.6	30.0
World War II			
(April 1945)	19,570,000	36.1	37.0
Pre-World War II			
(March 1940)	13,840,000	25.4	27.6
LONG-TERM TRENDS[2]			
1930 (April)	10,396,000	21.9	23.6
1920 (January)	8,229,000	20.4	22.7
1900 (June)	4,999,000	18.1	20.0
1890 (June)	3,704,000	17.0	18.2

SOURCE: U.S. Department of Labor, Bureau of Labor Statistics: *Employment and Earnings*, May 1965 and 1960. U.S. Department of Commerce, Bureau of the Census: *Annual Report on the Labor Force*, 1940-55. Social Science Research Council: "Labor Force in the United States, 1890-1960" (1948).

[1]Civilian labor force.

[2]Decennial census (total labor force).

Trends in Employment

Since 1940, American women have been responsible for the major share of growth in the labor force, accounting for more than 60 percent of the total increase from 1940 to 1964. Their representation in the labor force has risen from one fourth to more than one third of all workers. See Table IV.

Table IV

PERCENTAGE OF WOMEN IN TOTAL WORK FORCE

Year	Total Employees	Percent Women
1940	53,299,000	24.4
1945	65,300,000	29.6
1950	64,749,000	28.8
1955	68,887,000	29.2
1960	72,104,000	37.1
1965	77,177,000	38.8
1970*	84,617,000	40.5
1975*	92,183,000	41.3
1980*	99,942,000	41.9

SOURCE: *Statistical Abstract of the United States*, 1962 and 1968.

*Projected.

Major occupational groups

Employment of women has expanded in most major occupational groups since 1940. Women were reported in all of the 479 individual occupations listed in the 1960 decennial census. The occupations in the labor force are divided into eleven broad categories. More women were concentrated in clerical work than any other major occupational group; the next largest groups were service workers and operatives. Professional workers were fourth, with private-household, sales, and managerial workers following in that order. (See Table V.)

The latest census in 1960 also showed women concentrated in a relatively small number of occupations. Nearly one fourth of all employed were secretaries, saleswomen in retail trade, private household workers, and teachers in elementary schools (Table VI). About one third of all working women were in seven occupations—the four listed previously and bookkeeper, waitress, and professional nurse. In fact, nearly two thirds of the 21.2 million

18

Table V

MAJOR OCCUPATIONAL GROUPS OF EMPLOYED WOMEN, 1940,1950, 1965 [1]
(14 years of age and over)

Major occupational group	Number (in thousands)			As percent of total employed		
	1965	1950	1940	1965	1950	1940
Total	24,648	17,176	11,920	34.7	29.3	25.9
Professional, technical, kindred workers	3,323	1,862	1,570	37.4	41.8	45.4
Managers, officials, proprietors	1,106	941	450	14.8	14.8	11.7
Clerical, kindred workers..............	7,756	4,539	2,530	69.9	59.3	52.6
Sales workers	1,881	1,516	830	40.6	39.0	27.9
Craftsmen, foremen.......	281	181	110	3.2	2.4	2.1
Operatives	3,656	3,215	2,190	27.7	26.9	25.7
Laborers	116	68	100	3.2	2.2	3.2
Private-household	2,025	1,771	2,100	97.5	92.1	93.8
Service workers	3,829	2,168	1,350	54.8	45.4	40.1
Farmers, farm managers ...	140	253	690	6.0	5.5	8.0
Farm laborers, foremen....	534	663		29.5	27.4	

SOURCE: U.S. Department of Labor, Bureau of Labor Statistics.

[1] Data are for April of each year. (Not reported separately prior to 1940.)

women employed in 1960 were in 36 individual occupations, each of which engaged 100,000 or more women. About two fifths of these occupations were white-collar, one fourth manual, and the remainder were service.

The expanded participation of women in the labor force, however, appears not to have been accompanied by improved utilization of their abilities. Occupationally, women appear relatively more disadvantaged now than twenty-five years ago. In 1940 they held 45 percent of all professional and technical positions. In 1965 women held only 37 percent of such jobs. This decline has occurred despite women's total employment increase over the same period and the rising proportion of women college graduates.[1] In fact, many women hold jobs less than commensurate with their abilities and educational achievement. In March 1966, 7 percent of the women workers with five or more years of college were working as service workers, operatives, sales workers, or clerical workers. (See Chart II.)

Table VI

DETAILED OCCUPATIONS IN WHICH 100,000 OR MORE WOMEN
WERE EMPLOYED IN 1960
(14 years of age and over)

Occupation	Number	As percent of total employed
Secretaries	1,423,352	97
Saleswomen (retail trade)	1,397,364	54
Private-household workers	1,162,683	96
Teachers (elementary)	860,413	86
Bookkeepers	764,054	84
Waitresses	714,827	87
Nurses (professional)	567,884	98
Sewers and stitchers (mfg)	534,258	94
Typists	496,735	95
Cashiers	367,954	78
Cooks (except private household)	361,772	64
Telephone operators	341,797	96
Babysitters	319,735	98
Attendants	288,268	74
Laundry and drycleaning	277,396	72
Assemblers	270,769	44
Operatives (apparel and accessories)	270,619	75
Hairdressers (and cosmetologists)	267,050	89
Packers and wrappers	262,935	60
Stenographers	258,554	96
Teachers (secondary school)	243,452	47
Office machine operators	227,849	74
Checkers, examiners and inspectors	215,066	45
Practical nurses	197,115	96
Kitchen workers	179,796	59
Chambermaids and maids (except household)	162,433	98
Housekeepers (private household)	143,290	99
Operatives (electrical machinery, equipment and supplies)	138,001	48
Receptionists	131,142	98
Charwomen and cleaners	122,728	68
Housekeepers and stewardesses (except private household)	117,693	81
Dressmakers and seamstresses	115,252	97
Counter and fountain workers	112,547	71
File clerks	112,323	86
Musicians and music teachers	109,638	57
Operatives (yarn, thread and fabric mills)	103,399	44

SOURCE: U.S. Department of Commerce, Bureau of the Census: U.S. Census of Population, 1960.

The increased concentration of women in the lower paying occupations in the past decade is reflected in the widening gap between

CHART II

MANY WOMEN WORKERS ARE UNDERUTILIZED IN RELATION
TO THEIR EDUCATIONAL ACHIEVEMENT

(Percentage of Women With One or More Years of College Employed in
the Lesser Skilled Occupations, March 1965)

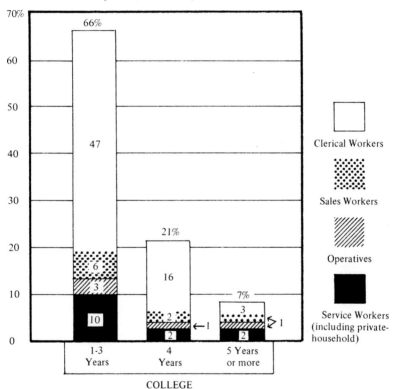

COLLEGE

Source: U.S. Department of Labor, Bureau of Labor Statistics.

the median (half above, half below) earnings of women and men.
In 1964 the median wage or salary income of women who worked
thirty-five hours or more a week and for fifty to fifty-two weeks
was only 60 percent that of men. In 1955 it had been 64 percent.
Of all women who worked year-round full-time in 1964, 32 percent
received incomes of less than $3,000 a year and only 6 percent had
incomes of $7,000 or more a year. (See Chart III.)

CHART III

ONE THIRD OF WOMEN WHO WORK YEAR ROUND FULL TIME* RECEIVE LESS THAN $3,000 A YEAR

(Percent Distribution of Year-Round Full-Time Workers, by Income and Sex, 1964)

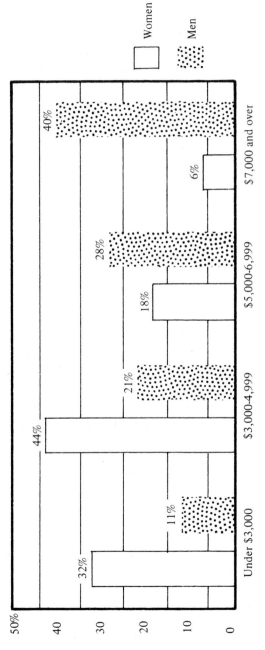

Source: U.S. Department of Commerce, Bureau of the Census.

*50 to 52 weeks a year, 35 hours or more a week.

22

Role in Management

More than one million women were employed as "proprietors, managers and officials" (except farm) in April 1965. This group had more than doubled in number since 1940, with most of the increase occurring prior to 1950. Nevertheless, this is a comparatively small occupational group for women; men outnumber them seven to one.[2]

Of the 2,200,000 "managers, officials and proprietors" listed by the U. S. Census as earning $10,000 or more per year, only a fraction, 55,000, are female. In 1965, *Fortune* magazine estimated that only about 2 percent of all "real" executives were women. There are few women who top the management in any of the major corporations, and one has to look very hard to find a female vice president. The executives in business say to women, "Yes, we want you. But we want you behind the typewriter."[3]

Former Equal Employment Opportunity Commission Chairman Clifford L. Alexander, Jr., stated that while an analysis by sex of statistical data from the 1966 official employer-reporting forms indicated women may fill nearly one-half of the total white-collar jobs in a given area, their representation is very small in higher echelon managerial and professional jobs.[4]

The Equal Employment Opportunity Commission did a study on employment opportunities for minorities among the fifteen top industries in New York City.[5] The Commission reported that women comprised 47 percent of the white-collar labor force. There was a large concentration of women in office and clerical occupations; they were only slightly underrepresented among technicians and salesworkers, but considerably underrepresented among officials and managers.

While educational attainment of women matched and surpassed that for males at every level in the white-collar hierarchy, 74 percent of the white-collar women workers were in clerical occupations; only about 10 percent were in managerial and professional positions.[6]

The Commission concluded that in many business areas a discriminatory attitude persists against hiring women regardless of their qualifications. Women continue to face many specific barriers with respect to initial appointment, assignment, training, and promotion.[7]

The federal government provides one of the more hospitable environments for the employment of educated women. But, despite the federal government's emphasis on opportunities for employment and advancement of women since 1964, there appears to be relatively little change in the number of women in upper level administrative positions in the career service. A comprehensive study of employment of women in the federal government conducted by the Civil Service Commission revealed a third of all government white-collar workers are women but only 2 percent hold key managerial positions. The study found women concentrated in lower grade levels and office positions. In 1967, of 1,932,510 full-time federal white-collar workers (in U. S. and abroad), 659,403 were women; 105,283 women were Grade 5 or above, and 15 had exceeded Grade 18.[8] Further, the report indicated that the administration of former President Johnson made a deliberate effort to elevate more women to senior executive status. Twenty-one women were appointed to executive jobs not previously held by women, and 200 more were appointed to presidential boards and commissions dealing with major national issues. All women in government service earning more than $30,289 a year in 1968 were appointees under the Johnson administration with the exception of Assistant Secretary of Labor Esther Peterson, who was selected by the late President Kennedy.

Reasons women are not hired for management positions

The Harvard Business School surveyed 1,000 businessmen in 1965 and found that 41 percent of them viewed women executives with "undisguised misgivings."[9] Attitudes among male executives range, according to a survey by *Dun's Review,* from extremes of "qualified women should perform adequately in any job" to "women are excellent in handling details, but never in management!" Old-line executives, especially, find it hard to discard the prejudices of a lifetime against mingling women and business. Even those executives who are much more liberal in recognizing ability in a woman are quick to agree that any woman who gets ahead in management has had to contend and will have to contend with much resentment and prejudice.

Commissioner Luther Holcomb, Equal Employment Opportunity Commission, said in 1968 the most crucial issue before EEOC now relates to the realm of sex. "We have lived in a period where a woman's place was at home in the kitchen or in bed," he said. "If she worked she was a teacher. Our tradition has been to employ a lady because we could get her cheaper." Dr. Holcomb further commented that American businessmen should take the pulse of what is happening in civil rights in this nation and begin putting women in responsible positions before the government has to step in to protect women's employment rights.[10]

Attitudes and prejudices deeply rooted in tradition and custom are not easily overcome. The idea that woman's place is only in the home still prevails among many in our society. An executive may be proud of his secretary, but she rarely gets the promotion. The general attitude is that men have careers, but women who work only have jobs. They are not permanent; they are just working for another car or to help put the children through college or make a down payment on a new house.

Then there are the general social concerns. Society speculates about how employment of married women may affect husband-wife relationships and the welfare of children. Society wonders whether there is a relationship between the rising rate in juvenile delinquency and the working, absent-from-home mother.

Although reasons given by many employers for deciding not to hire women as executives are varied, they may be generally couched in the following beliefs:

Women will not stay on the payroll long enough to justify training expense. Some personnel directors report that, when compared with men, turnover among women is too high, and even if they may be good candidates for management positions they marry and have children. Many of the women who plan to take time out to have children do not return. After marriage, women do not have as much mobility as men. A male executive expects his wife to follow him when he is transferred, but a woman cannot expect her husband to follow her if she is transferred. These personnel directors contend a company cannot afford to invest in women. They cannot depend on women to remain in the labor market long enough to get any return on their investment. For this reason, women are excluded from most management training programs.

Women lack needed skills, training, education, for management positions. Women are disproportionately concentrated in the lesser skilled, less rewarding, and less rewarded occupations.

Many of these women are overqualified for the jobs they hold. The educational backgrounds of a great many women are not fully utilized in industry. More than one fifth of employed women with four years of college and two thirds of those who had completed one to three years of college were employed as service workers, operatives, sales workers, or clerical workers in 1965. A survey conducted by the Administrative Management Society among 1,900 business and industrial firms, published in 1961, showed that more than half of the respondents indicated they would choose a man instead of a woman when a higher office position becomes vacant, although both workers may be equally qualified.

Women are less productive. Many executives contend that women do not plan a long working career and, therefore, do not necessarily aspire to higher levels of responsibility at work. Women, this argument holds, would rather stay in a minor position where they have limited responsibility.

Women are absent from work more often than men. Many employers feel that the problem of absenteeism is complicated by the fact that women are likely to be called on to help if someone else in the family is ill. Women's dual responsibility in the home and on the job can create problems. However, in general, skill levels, salary, and responsibility seem to be more pertinent factors than sex in absenteeism. Aggregate statistics for 1960 show that average days lost due to chronic illness were 3.1 for men compared to 2.6 for women. The Public Health Service found that women average 5.4 days of sick leave and men 5.6 days.[11]

Men and women alike resent working for a woman. Most companies prefer not to place a woman supervisor in charge of a department with male workers because, they assume, rightly or wrongly, men do not like to work for women and women do not like working for women. Some men and women feel women are poorly qualified for supervisory positions because women are more emotional than men. Also, women are believed by some to have exaggerated preciseness, patronizing attitudes, and exclusively subjective judgments.[12] There is little tangible evidence to prove or disprove women are more irrational than men. While much has been written about women in industry, there are few scientific studies on the personality and psychological problems peculiar to the woman worker or woman manager.

Summary

In America the major change in the pattern of women's lives occurred after the Civil War with accelerating industrialization and urbanization. Increasingly, city women grew up without experience in work outside the home, particularly after they married and started their families. This isolation of women from work was a significant phenomenon in American life for about eighty years—from the Civil War to World War II. During this period, however, many women from lower income groups continued to work, usually in factories or as domestics. During World War II and since, women from the middle and upper classes entered the labor market with increasing momentum and now comprise one third of the total labor force.

Three conclusive factors emerge as one reviews the social and economic development in the evolution of the status of women from the Civil War period through the 1960's:

1. *Social agitation put the problem in perspective and ultimately resulted in Title VII of the Civil Rights Act.* The revolution in the woman's role outside the home did not just happen because the woman decided to abandon her domesticity. Many factors were responsible: growth and change in the economy, advances in science and technology, an expanding urban population, developments in education, the role of the government as an employer, the crisis situations of war and depression, social values and attitudes, patterns of marriage, childbearing, and life expectancy. These changes abruptly upset the expected, traditional role for women. Inevitably, many ambitious women became attracted by the challenge of business. We continue to experience the evolution of our society toward man-woman equality with only one basic differentiating factor: *ability.*

Legislation has helped women, providing more equal opportunity in job competition, pay, and advancement. Title VII of the Civil Rights Act of 1964, which requires that all employees be treated without regard to sex in every phase of employment, focused public attention on the status of women in business. Many women feel, however, the provision has not made any significant difference at the management level. The majority of sex discrimination complaints filed with the EEOC are at the blue-collar level where clear-cut union classifications protect the complainant. Nonunionized white-collar workers appear less anxious to bring a discrimination suit. It is apparently very difficult to prove a specific woman is more qualified than a specific man for a job at the management level.

2. *Women, while accepted in the work force, are still only semi-accepted in management.* Sociologists, psychologists, and other social scientists say old prejudices of male superiority have conditioned many women and men against women functioning in business at executive levels, and that women are deficient in emotional and intellectual abilities required by the demanding competitiveness of business. Further, the biological role of women has been used as justification for the traditional attitude "woman's place is in the home"; or, if she must work, certainly a woman's primary commitment is to the family, not a career.

In the past, economics has been a determining factor toward acceptance of women in business. Industrialization, World War II, and postwar factors, such as expansion of industry, the Korean conflict, the Vietnam conflict, shortages in scientific-technical fields, have contributed to the greater utilization of women.

3. *There is a shortage of management people in all functional areas, both line and staff.* Statistical evidence indicates that industry, government, and the professions may have to draw increasingly on women to fill manpower shortages. Inevitably, it appears that deep-rooted ideas about sexual roles will be modified as we experience the need for full integration of women into business at all levels.

Chapter IV

TITLE VII OF THE CIVIL RIGHTS ACT OF 1964

The principal purpose of the Civil Rights Act of 1964 was to eliminate discriminatory practices against Negroes. On February 8, 1964, however, an amendment to the Civil Rights Act, Title VII, prohibiting sex discrimination in private employment was approved by the United States Congress. This amendment gave the woman worker the right to compete for any job for which she is qualified. By forbidding employment discrimination against women in hiring, firing, promotion, and pay scale because of sex, Title VII brought many changes and opportunities for the woman worker, many of which opened doors traditionally closed to her. But, perhaps surprisingly, the sex amendment, in spite of existing sex discrimination in private employment, was not intended as corrective legislation. Rather, it was an attempt by conservative forces in Congress to confuse the application of Title VII toward providing equality for the Negro.

How Women Came to be Included

As information presented in chapters two and three indicated, it has been society's contention that the "woman's place is in the home." If economic necessity dictated she venture into the economic world, she had to work for lower salaries and with less chance for advancement than men in the same type jobs. Employment opportunity preferences were given to the male worker even if he were not more qualified.

Dissatisfaction with these prejudices eventually prompted women workers to organize and demand equal rights. However, many of their protests went unnoticed until the report of the President's Committee on the economic status of the woman worker was presented in 1963. The committee pointed up discriminatory practices against the woman worker and recommended equal opportunities in hiring, training, promotion, and pay, as well as improvement in minimum wage laws and other labor legislation affecting women. During the same year, the equal pay bill was passed. In 1964, the Civil Rights Act was passed by Congress, and Title VII, Section 703, specifically prohibited discrimination for reasons of race, creed, color, national origin, age, physical disability, political affiliation, and sex.

The federal government's authority to enact such legislation had been a slow evolvement. Slavery was abolished in 1865, but Congress's power to order social, economic, and political equality was held by the courts as unconstitutional until the 1930's. The Great Depression helped accelerate a legal end to discrimination. The Unemployment Relief Act (1933) prohibited discrimination based on race, color, or creed in federal employment, employment by government contractors, and training and placement opportunities provided by government funds. In 1941, the Fair Employment Practices Commission, established by President Franklin D. Roosevelt's Executive Order 8802, reaffirmed the principle of nondiscrimination in all government-supported or -sponsored activities. The second Fair Employment Practices Commission (1945-1946, Executive Order 9346) extended the government's surveillance to recruitment and training for war production and union membership.

Despite the action of the Executive branch in this area, Congress obstructed almost every discrimination bill concerning private employment from 1943 to 1964. From 1954 to 1963, only one of 120 fair employment proposals emerged from committee for debate on the Senate floor.[1] During President Eisenhower's administration, a fair employment practices proposal was considered along with the voting-rights-oriented Civil Rights Act of 1960. The voting-rights section was enacted; the Fair Employment Practices provisions were not.

During the Kennedy administration, Senator Hubert Humphrey (D, Minn.) introduced civil rights legislation (Senate bill 1937) proposing enforcement of equal employment opportunities by an administrative board under the Department of Labor.

Sex issue

The issue of sex discrimination first entered into discussion on February 3, 1964, when Congressman John Dowdy (D, Texas) introduced an amendment to the Public Accommodations section (Title II) of the proposed Civil Rights Act of 1964 adding sex to the proposed list of discriminatory classifications. This amendment was defeated. Congressman Dowdy then offered his sex amendment for inclusion in Title IV, which provided for the desegregation of public education. This amendment was also defeated.

February 8, 1964, House Rules Chairman Howard Smith offered an amendment to Title VII, the Federal Fair Employment Prac-

tices provision. Congressman Smith of Virginia in his proposal
said:

> .. this amendment is offered to the fair employment prac-
> tices title of this bill to include within our desire to prevent
> discrimination against another minority group, the women,
> but a very essential minority group, in the absence of which
> the majority group would not be here today.

> Now, I am very serious about this amendment. It has been
> offered at inappropriate places in the bill. Now, this is the
> appropriate place for this amendment to come in. I do not
> think it can do any harm to this legislation; maybe it can do
> some good. I think it will do some good for the minority sex.

> I think we all recognize and it is indisputable fact that all
> throughout industry women are discriminated against in that
> just generally speaking they do not get as high compensation
> for their work as do the majority sex. Now, if that is true, I
> hop that the committee chairman will accept this amend-
> ment.[2]

To illustrate how some of the women felt about discrimination
against them, Congressman Smith presented an extract from a
letter he had recently received:

> I suggest that you might also favor an amendment or a bill
> to correct the present "imbalance" which exists between males
> and females in the United States.

> The census of 1960 shows that we had 88,331,00 males living
> in this country, and 90,992,000 females, which leaves the coun-
> try with an "imbalance" of 2,661,000 females.

> Just why the Creator would set up such an imbalance of spin-
> sters, shutting off the "right" of every female to have a hus-
> band of her own, is, of course, known only to nature.

> But I am sure you will agree that this is a grave injustice to
> womankind and something the Congress and President Johnson
> should take immediate steps to correct, especially in this elec-
> tion year.[3]

Congressman Cellar from Virginia rose in opposition to the
amendment, citing a letter from Assistant Secretary of Labor,

Esther Peterson (then Director of the Women's Bureau), in support of his opposition:

> ... This question of broadening civil rights legislation to prohibit discrimination based on sex has arisen previously. The President's Commission on the Status of Women gave this matter careful consideration in its discussion of Executive Order 10925 which now prohibits discrimination based on race, creed, color, or national origin in employment under Federal contracts. Its conclusion is stated on page 30 of its report "American Women," as follows:
>
>> We are aware that this order could be expanded to forbid discrimination based on sex. But discrimination based on sex, the Commission believes, involves problems sufficiently different from discrimination based on the other factors listed to make separate treatment preferable.
>
> In view of this policy conclusion reached by representatives from a variety of women's organizations and private and public agencies to attack discrimination based on sex separately, we are of the opinion that to so amend H. R. 7152 would not be to the best advantage of women at this time.[4]

Congressman Cellar went on to say:

> ... At first blush it seems fair, just and equitable to grant these equal rights. But when you examine carefully what the import and repercussions are concerning equal rights throughout American life you run into a considerable amount of difficulty ....
>
> ... Imagine the upheaval that would result from adoption of blanket language requiring total equality. Would male citizens be justified in insisting that women share with them the burdens of compulsory military service? What would become of traditional family relationships? What about alimony? Who would have the obligation of supporting whom? Would fathers rank equally with mothers in the rights of custody to children? What would become of the crimes of rape and statutory rape? Would the Mann Act be invalidated? Would the many state and local provisions regulating working conditions and hours of employment for women be struck down?

You know the biological differences between the sexes. In many states we have laws favorable to women. Are you going to strike those laws down? ...The list of foreseeable consequences, I will say to the committee, is unlimited.

What is more, even conceding that some degree of discrimination against women obtains in the area of employment, it is contrary to the situation with respect to civil rights for Negroes. Real and genuine progress is being made in discrimination against women. The Equal Pay Act of 1963, for example, which became law last June, amends the Fair Labor Standards Act of 1938 by prohibiting discrimination between employees on the basis of sex, with respect to wages for equal work on jobs requiring equal skills, effort and responsibility.[5]

Congressman Cellar further called the amendment "illogical, ill-timed, ill-placed, and improper." With the exception of Congresswoman Edith Green (D, Oregon), the women in Congress supported Smith's amendment. Frances P. Bolton (D, Ohio) was first to rise in support of the amendment. However, she proposed to offer an amendment to Title X, the miscellaneous title. Congressman Smith responded that he did not like the idea of placing the amendment under "miscellaneous." "I think women are entitled to more dignity than that," he said.

Congresswoman Martha Griffith (D, Mich.) then rose in support of the amendment, stating she supported the amendment because "I feel as a white woman when this bill has passed this House and the Senate and has been signed by the President that white women will be last at the hiring gate." She further noted that the Swedish sociologist, Gunnar Myrdal, in *The American Dilemma,* pointed out twenty years ago that "white women and Negroes occupied relatively the same position in American society."

Congresswoman Griffith went on to say:

If you do not add sex to this bill, I really do not believe there is a reasonable person sitting here who does not by now understand perfectly that you are going to have white men in one bracket, you are going to try to take colored men and colored women and give them equal employment rights and down at the bottom of the list is going to be a white woman with no rights at all.

33

Congresswoman Griffith expressed ". . .a vote against this amendment today by a white man is a vote against his wife, or his widow, or his daughter, or his sister. If we are trying to establish equality in jobs, I am for it, but I am for making white women equal, also." Katherine St. George (D, New York) supported the sex amendment. In responding to Mr. Cellar's consideration of the amendment as illogical, she said:

> I can think of nothing more logical than this amendment at this point. . . . Why should women be denied equality of opportunity? Why should women be denied equal pay for equal work?
>
> We do not want special privileges. We do not need special privileges. We outlast you—we outlive you—we nag you to death. So why should we want special privileges? I believe that we can hold our own. We are entitled to this little crumb of equality.
>
> The addition of that little, terrifying word "s-e-x" will not hurt this legislation in any way. In fact, it will improve it. It will make it comprehensive. It will make it logical. It will make it right.

Congresswoman Edith Green (D, Oregon) author of the Equal Pay Act of 1963 and a member of the President's Commission on the Status of Women, was the only congresswoman to oppose the amendment. Congresswoman Green did not believe this was the time or place for the amendment. She felt the main purpose of the legislation was to help end discrimination practiced against Negroes in voting, public accommodations, education, and employment. She said:

> . . .As much as I hope the day will come when discrimination will be ended against women, I really and sincerely hope that this amendment will not be added to this bill. It will clutter up the bill and it may later—very well—be used to help destroy this section of the bill by some of the very people who today support it. And I hope that no other amendment will be added to this bill on sex or age or anything else, that would jeopardize our primary purpose in any way.

In further support of her position, Congresswoman Green read a letter she had received from the American Association of University Women:

Honorable Edith Green
House of Representatives
Washington, D. C.

Dear Mrs. Green:

It has been brought to the attention of the Legislative Program Committee of the American Association of University Women, which is meeting today, that it is probable that an amendment providing for the addition of the word "sex" to section 704 in title 7 of the Civil Rights bill on discrimination because of race, color, religion or national origin would be offered on the floor this afternoon. In our opinion the inclusion of the word "sex" in this title on discrimination is redundant and could actually work to the disadvantage of this very important legislation. We urge you to speak against this and other amendments which could weaken or impede the passage of this very vital legislation which you, as an AAUW member, know we in the association support.

Sincerely,

Marjorie C. Hahn
Chairman, Legislative
Program Committee

Congresswoman Catherine May (D, Washington) in supporting the amendment, stressed that Esther Peterson's letter in opposition to the amendment did not speak for all women of the United States nor for all university women. She said:

I share the views of my colleague from Oregon in her desire to eliminate the proven discrimination which colored women have suffered, but at the same time I feel it is only just and fair to give all women protection against discrimination.

After a week of debate and numerous attacks on other sections of the bill, the sex amendment was approved by a vote of 168-133. On February 10, 1964, the House of Representatives approved H. R. 7152, the Civil Rights Act of 1964, by a vote of 230-130.

Although passage of the Civil Rights Act of 1964 was a significant defeat for the southern Democrats and Republican conservatives, the inclusion of the sex amendment was a notable achievement. With the amendment, they felt that they had a powerful weapon with which to wreck the application of Title VII.[6]

The Act

The ban on discriminatory employment practices (Title VII) became effective July 2, 1965. It applies to all phases of the employer-employee relationship such as recruiting, hiring, training, upgrading, and promotion policies, and any other conditions or privileges of employment. Employers and unions with one hundred or more workers in any industry were immediately affected. On July 2, 1968, the law was extended to include employers and unions with as few as twenty-five workers.

Four major groups are affected by the Act: employers, public and private employment agencies, labor organizations, and joint labor-management apprenticeship programs. Those not covered by the Act include local, state and federal agencies, government-owned corporations, Indian tribes, and educational institutions where the employee performs work connected with the institution's educational activities.[7]

The Act states specifically (in part):

It shall be an unlawful employment practice for an employer

(1) to fail or refuse to hire or to discharge any individual, or otherwise to discriminate against any individual with respect to his compensation, terms, conditions, or privileges, of employment, because of such individual's race, color, religion, sex or nation origin; or

(2) to limit, segregate or classify his employees in any way which would deprive or tend to deprive any individual of employment opportunities or otherwise adversely affect his status as an employee, because of such individual's race, color, religion, sex, or national origin.[8]

The Equal Employment Opportunity Commission

Title VII established the Equal Employment Opportunity Commission (EEOC), composed of five members appointed by the President and approved by the Senate, to administer the law and to receive, investigate; and conciliate employment discrimination charges under Title VII. The Commission's responsibility is to assure that all Americans will be considered for hiring and promotion on the basis of their ability and qualifications, without regard to race, color, religion, sex, or national origin.

Specifically, the Commission has the power to:

(1) cooperate with and, with their consent, use regional, state,

local and other agencies, both public and private, and individuals;

(2) furnish technical assistance to persons subject to the law who ask for it to further their compliance with the law or any order issued under it;

(3) furnish conciliation services at the request of an employer or union whose employees or members refuse to cooperate in carrying out the provisions of the law;

(4) make such technical studies as may be appropriate to carry out the purposes of the law and make the results of its studies available to the public;

(5) refer matters to the Attorney General with recommendations that he (a) intervene in a civil action brought by a person discriminated against or (b) start civil suit where there's a pattern of discrimination in violation of the law. Commission may advise, consult and assist the Attorney General on such matters.

The Commission has no authority to start suit. Its primary purpose is to secure voluntary adjustment of unlawful employment practice complaints. Its powers are limited to consulting and advising. The chairman of the Commission is authorized to appoint officers, agents, attorneys, and employees to assist the Commission in carrying out its duties. Also, the Commission may cooperate with state and local agencies that administer state or local fair employment practices laws and may use the services of these agencies. It may enter into agreements with these state and local agencies, dealing with the right to sue (ceding jurisdiction over complaints to these agencies wherever the practice complained of also violates state or local law).

The basic purpose of the Civil Rights Act was to ensure equality for all citizens:

To enforce the constitutional right to vote, to confer jurisdiction upon the district courts of the United States to provide injunctive relief against discrimination in public accommodations, to authorize the Attorney General to institute suits to protect constitutional rights in public facilities and public education, to extend the Commission on Civil Rights, to prevent discrimination in federally assisted programs, to establish a Commission on Equal Employment Opportunity, and for other purposes.[9]

37

Title VII prohibits the following unlawful employment practices:

(1) For employers—failure or refusal to hire; discharges; any other discrimination with respect to pay, or terms or conditions of employment; limiting, segregating, or classifying employees in any way which deprives them of or adversely affects their status;

(2) For employment agencies—failure or refusal to refer for employment; or to classify or refer for employment on any of the prohibited discriminatory bases;

(3) For labor unions—the exclusion or expelling of members; the limiting, segregating, or classification of members; and failure or refusal to refer for employment in any way which deprives them of or adversely affects their status;

(4) For employers, labor unions, or joint labor-management committees controlling an apprenticeship or job training program—denial of admission to or employment in any program established to provide apprenticeship or other training, and publication of advertisements or notices indicating a preference;

(5) Anyone retaliating against an individual for invoking the law's processes, or assisting others in doing so, or publishing advertisements stating a preference for workers in one sex except where sex is a bona fide occupational qualification for employment.[10]

In November, 1965, a new guideline interpretation on the sex discrimination provision included (1) conflict between state protective laws for women and Title VII, (2) classified advertising and bona fide occupational qualification, and (3) responsibility of employment agencies.

Procedure for filing complaints

If a person believes he has a discrimination complaint against an employer, labor organization, employment agency, or joint labor-management program for apprenticeship or training, he may file a complaint with the Commission. The EEOC accepts these complaints, investigates the charges, checks employer records, and gets written testimony. After checking the records, if the Commission finds evidence of valid discrimination, it tries to negotiate a voluntary settlement with the employer-offender. These actions could result in job applicants being hired with retroactive wages. The employee may get a pay raise or promotion that had earlier been denied. If the negotiation fails, the worker may file a civil suit.

Although several cases have been tried and decisions made in favor of the woman worker, many of the problems are being solved without court action through negotiation between employers and the Commission. In a survey of 423 companies employing 954,000 workers, conducted to measure progress of employers' compliance with Title VII between mid-1965 and 1966, the following was revealed:

(1) Three out of every ten companies have made changes in policies to help reduce sex discrimination.

(2) More companies now give maternity leaves.

(3) Male and female seniority lists have been eliminated in many companies.

(4) One fourth of the companies have eliminated the "male only" jobs.[11]

Summary

The sex provision of Title VII of the Civil Rights Act of 1964 was not originally proposed to alleviate women's employment disadvantage. Rather, its primary purpose was to impede the passage, and later application of the Civil Rights Act.

The Equal Employment Opportunity Commission was established to administer the law to assure equal consideration for all individuals on the sole basis of ability.

Chapter V

ACTIONS BROUGHT UNDER TITLE VII

The Unemployment Relief Act in 1933 first enunciated the principle of equal job opportunity; and the Fair Labor Standards Act of 1938, popularly known as the "Federal Wages and Hours Act," is the nation's first federal law on wages of men, women, and minors working in interstate commerce. In 1941 President Franklin D. Roosevelt established the Fair Employment Practices Commission to "encourage full participation in the national defense program by all citizens of the United States, regardless of race, creed, color, or national origin." The second Fair Employment Commission (1943) extended government surveillance to recruitment and training for war production and union membership.

Not until 1961, however, when President Kennedy established the President's Commission on the Status of Women, was attention refocused on women in the labor market. Two years later, in 1963, the Equal Pay Act amending the Fair Labor Standard's Act of 1938 was passed; and in 1964 Title VII of the Civil Rights Act was enacted.

Title VII of the Civil Rights Act caused employers to examine existing employment practices. As a result, many companies found their policies conflicted with the equal opportunity provisions of Title VII. Often, women's employment was restricted on the basis of marriage and age. In many states, legislation prohibited or restricted women's employment. Training women for managerial positions was not considered profitable by many employers. The conflicts ran the gamut of employment relationships and included classified advertising, recruitment hire, transfer, promotion, layoff, discharge, job classifications, wages and salaries, seniority, maternity leave, retirement age, insurance and pension benefits, and physical disability coverage.

Complaints of Discrimination

In the first year of Equal Employment Opportunity Commission's existence (July 2, 1965 to June 30, 1966), 8,854 discrimination charges were filed; and from July 1, 1966, to June 30, 1967, 9,688 new charges were received. Official statistics indicate a total of 10,095, 12,148, and 14,129 new charges for 1968, 1969, and 1970, respectively. Sex discrimination charges constituted about 20 percent of these complaints.

Of the 28,637 new charges received between July 2, 1965, and June 30, 1968, 14,913 qualified for investigation. Of these, 4,271 were deferred for state or local Fair Employment Practices Commission action, and additional information was required for 6,633. There were 10,634 which did not come under the Equal Employment Opportunity Commission's jurisdiction. Investigations were completed for 10,576. At the end of the first year's operation,

Table VII

DISPOSITION OF COMPLAINTS BROUGHT BEFORE THE
EQUAL EMPLOYMENT OPPORTUNITY COMMISSION
JULY 2, 1965 TO JUNE 30, 1970

	1965-66	1966-67	1967-68	1968-69	1969-70	Total
New charges received	8,854	9,688	10,095	12,148	14,129	54,914
Charges recommended for investigation	3,773	5,084	6,056	9,152	11,255	35,320
Charges deferred for state or local FEPC action	977	1,158	2,136	2,980	4,201	11,452
Charges requiring additional information	1,383	2,270	2,980	2,339	2,324	11,296
No probable jurisdiction	2,063	4,415	3,886	2,801	2,342	15,507
Completed investigation	1,659	3,549	5,368	7,543	5,090	23,209
Pending investigation	2,114	2,796	3,484	5,093	11,258	24,745

SOURCE: First, Second, Third, Fourth, and Fifth Annual Reports, Equal Employment Opportunity Commission, Washington, D.C., 1965-1970.

June 30, 1966, 2,114 charges were pending investigations; 2,796 complaints were pending at the end of the second year's operation, June 30, 1967; 3,484 charges were pending investigation at the end of the third year's operation June 30, 1968; 5,093 charges were pending investigation at the end of the fourth year's operation June 30, 1969; and, 11,258 complaints were pending investigation at the end of the fifth year's operation June 30, 1970.[2] (See Table VII for a statistical breakdown.)

Follow-up

Charges must be filed with the Equal Employment Opportunity Commission within ninety days after the occurrence of the conduct under complaint. These charges may be initiated in either of two ways: (1) A charge may be filed in writing and under oath by an individual claiming to be aggrieved; or (2) a written charge may be filed with the Equal Employment Opportunity Commission by a member of the Commission who has reasonable cause to believe that a violation has occurred. Also, a Commissioner's charge may be filed for an individual who has a legitimate charge but, for special reasons, wishes to remain anonymous.

If the state has a Fair Employment Practices Law, the Commission may not accept an individual complaint until the state authorities have received notice of the charge and have been given sixty days in which to act. If the state fair employment practices agency's action is not satisfactory, the individual may file a complaint with the Commission within thirty days after completion of the state or local proceedings.

After a charge is filed, the Commission must furnish the accused (employer, employment agency, or labor organization) with a copy of the charge. The Commission may then make an investigation. The charge, however, is not made public by the Commission.

The Commission, when investigating a charge, may examine witnesses under oath and require production of documentary evidence. If there is sufficient evidence to support the charge, the Commission attempts to eliminate the alleged unlawful practice by conciliation. If these conciliatory efforts are unsuccessful, the aggrieved party is notified and within thirty days, if it wishes to pursue the charge, must institute civil suit in the federal district court. The claimant when filing suit with the district court must meet two preliminary filing requisites: (1) prior filing of a complaint with the Equal Employment Opportunity Commission within thirty days of the claimed action of discrimination; and (2) receipt from the Equal Employment Opportunity Commission of a letter indicating that evidence exists to indicate the law has been violated.

If the court finds the employer, employment agency, or labor organization has intentionally practiced unlawful employment procedures, the court can enjoin the unlawful activity and order appropriate affirmative action. Failure to comply with the court order subjects the accused either to criminal contempt proceedings and upon conviction a fine up to $1,000 and/or imprisonment up to six months; or to civil contempt proceedings where the defendant may be assessed so many dollars a day for each day's continuing violation of the court's order. In the criminal contempt proceedings, the accused is entitled to a jury trial, but a civil contempt proceeding does not carry that privilege. If the offending party fails to comply with the court order issued in the civil action, the Commission may begin court proceedings through the Justice Department and the Attorney General in the United States District Court.

Legislation is before Congress which would provide the Equal Employment Opportunity Commission with the power, after unsuccessful conciliatory efforts, "to issue a complaint, hold a hearing with the charging party and respondent appearing as parties to the action and, upon finding unlawful employment practices, to issue a cease and desist order to eliminate the practice. If no unlawful practice were found, the Commission would issue an order dismissing the charge."[3]

Conciliation

The Commission has reached agreements with most employers through conciliation. Many large employers such as Western Electric, IBM, Lockheed, and Southern Bell, immediately after Title VII became legally applicable July 2, 1965, affirmed their cooperation with the Equal Employment Opportunity Commission by incorporating equal employment opportunity statements into their formal operating policies. For example, Western Electric in a public statement regarding its company policy and organization said:

> While the Western Electric Company has long been committed to the concept and practice of Equal Employment Opportunity for minority citizens throughout the country, the Company's current policy of aggressive affirmative action is a matter of record epitomized by the Plan for Progress agreement signed on July 21, 1961. This agreement provides an unequivocal statement of the Company's philosophy:
>
>> It is the policy of the Western Electric Company that all applicants for employment and all employees are recruited, hired and assigned on the basis of merit without discrimination because of race, creed, color, or national origin. The employment policies and practices of the Western Electric Company have been and will continue to be such to insure that all of its employees are treated equally and that no distinctions are made in rates of pay, opportunities for advance-

ment, including upgrading, promotion and transfer because of the employee's color, religious belief or national origin. In terms of company policy this statement from our Plan for Progress agreement has been amended to affirm our longstanding belief in Equal Employment Opportunity for all employees regardless of sex or age.

It is the responsibility of every manager and supervisor in the company to implement this policy. To insure and facilitate this implementation we have provided our managers with strong staff support at the highest levels. At the time of the signing of the Plan for Progress the staff responsibility for the development and dissemination of the Company's Equal Employment policies and executive actions on a corporate basis was assigned to the Vice President, Personnel and Labor Relations. He was assisted in carrying out these responsibilities by a competent staff including the Company Personnel Director, the Director of Personnel Administration and the Manager of Personnel Administration. This Manager, in addition to his other functions, was charged with the task of establishing and administering procedures and programs in conformity with the provisions of Company policy, the Joint Statement on the Plan for Progress, Executive Orders of the President of the United States and all applicable statutes on non-discrimination. The Manager served as the major consultant on Equal Employment Opportunity for all Company organizations and coordinated the Company's relationship with various government agencies. He was also responsible for disseminating information on policy and procedures to all employees and particularly to those responsible for Equal Employment Opportunity at all of our locations.

In order to further strengthen this organization, we have recently made a basic change. The Company has now appointed a new fourth level supervisor in the organization of the Vice President whose sole responsibility will be the development and administration of Corporate Equal Employment policy. He will devote his full energies to Equal Employment and his functions will include all of the matters in this area previously handled by the Manager, Personnel Administration. In addition, he will have an important new function. His organization will be responsible for the systematic survey of every company location throughout the country to insure total adherence to the Company Equal Employment policy.

... In order to make all of our employees knowledgeable in this area, we have prepared detailed Company instructions and forwarded them to all locations. These are updated whenever it is appropriate and necessary to do so. The Company policy statements are similarly distributed to all supervisors so that our employees are kept abreast of our commitment and concern.[4]

Likewise, many employers, as illustrated in Table VIII, have cooperated with the Equal Employment Opportunity Commission, formally outlining their equal opportunity employment policies and operating practices to their employees and settling legitimate discriminatory charges through arbitration.

Table VIII

CONCILIATORY ACTIVITY UNDER THE EQUAL EMPLOYMENT
COMMISSION, JULY 2, 1965 TO JUNE 30, 1970

Analysis of Completed Conciliations	1965-66	1966-67	1967-68	1968-69	1969-70	Total
Fully successful	156	306	424	486	342	1,714
Partially successful	27	77	89	90	105	388
Unsuccessful	76	507	731	729	732	2,782
Pending	658	933	1,262	2,024	1,097	5,974

SOURCE: *First, Second, Third, Fourth, and Fifth Annual Reports*, Equal Employment Opportunity Commission, Washington, D.C., 1965-70.

Sex Discrimination Complaints

Sex complaints, as broken down by the Equal Employment Opportunity Commission, fall into the general categories of hiring, discharge, compensation, terms, conditions, classification, and miscellaneous. Further, the Commission classified its actions on sex complaints into five types:

(1) Charges which are deferred for state or local FEPC action.
(2) Charges for which more information is required.
(3) Charges over which the Equal Employment Opportunity Commission has no jurisdiction.
(4) Charges which are closed, withdrawn, or pending reanalysis.
(5) Charges which are recommended for investigation.

45

1965-1966

Of 8,854 discrimination matters received, 6,133 were recommended for investigations, deferred, or additional information required; 2,053 were sex discrimination charges. Of these sex discrimination complaints, 1,624 were recommended for investigation (See Table IX).

Table IX

ANALYSIS OF SEX DISCRIMINATION COMPLAINT ACTION BY
EQUAL EMPLOYMENT OPPORTUNITY COMMISSION
1965-1966

Total complaints received	8,854
Sex discrimination complaints	2,053
Recommended for investigation	1,624
Deferred for state or local FEP action	129
Additional information required	300

SOURCE: *First Annual Report*, Equal Employment Opportunity Commission, Washington, D.C.

Table X shows a breakdown of these complaints and statistics for each category.

1966-1967

During this period, the Equal Employment Opportunity Commission's total caseload was 12,927; new charges received were 9,688. Of 8,512 charges either recommended for investigation, deferred for state or local FEPC action, or returned for additional information, 2,003 pertained to sex. Of 1,932 charges for which there was no probable jurisdiction, 238 pertained to sex. These charges were directed at employer practices, union practices, employment agency practices, labor-management practices, and employer-union-agency practices. Table XI shows the statistical breakdown of the employment problem areas.

1967-1968

Of 11,172 charges either recommended for investigation, deferred for state or local FEPC action, or returned for additional information, 2,410 pertained to sex discrimination. A statistical breakdown for each complaint category is given in Table XII.

1968-1969

In this fiscal year, 14,471 charges were either recommended for

Table X

CLASSIFICATION OF SEX DISCRIMINATION COMPLAINTS RECEIVED BY THE EQUAL EMPLOYMENT OPPORTUNITY COMMISSION DURING FIRST YEAR OF OPERATION 1965-66

Nature of Problems Alleged:

Hiring		170
men	35	
women	135	
Promotion		97
Job classification		213
Wage differential		93
Benefits		726
Do not hire women with children		4
Do not hire women as trainees		4
Layoff, recall, and seniority		291
Fire women when marry		45
Fire women when have children		4
Fire women and replace with men		47
Age limitation for women		31
Job opportunities-advertising		9
State labor laws for women		291
overtime	262	
weight	16	
rest periods	2	
general allegations	11	
Union refusal to process grievances		12
Employment agency referral		9
Miscellaneous		80
Firing (unexplained)		9

SOURCE: Equal Employment Opportunity Commission, First Annual Report, 1965-66.

Table XI

CLASSIFICATION OF SEX DISCRIMINATION COMPLAINTS RECEIVED BY THE EQUAL EMPLOYMENT OPPORTUNITY COMMISSION, 1966-1967

Total Sex Discrimination Charges		2,003
Employer Practices		1,674
Hiring		194
women	174	
men	20	

continued

Table XI
(continued)

```
Discharge . . . . . . . . . . . . . . . . . . . . . . 230
            women . . . . . . . . 217
            men  . . . . . . . . . 13
Compensation  . . . . . . . . . . . . . . . . . . . . 262
            women . . . . . . . . 256
            men  . . . . . . . . .  6
Terms . . . . . . . . . . . . . . . . . . . . . . . . 424
            women . . . . . . . . 393
            men  . . . . . . . . . 31
Conditions  . . . . . . . . . . . . . . . . . . . . . 216
            women . . . . . . . . 188
            men  . . . . . . . . . 28
Classification . . . . . . . . . . . . . . . . . . . . 323
            women . . . . . . . . 313
            men  . . . . . . . . . 10
Miscellaneous  . . . . . . . . . . . . . . . . . . . .  25
            women . . . . . . . . 23
            men  . . . . . . . . .  2

Union Practices . . . . . . . . . . . . . . . . . . . . . . . . . . . . 208
            Discrimination . . . . . . . . . . . . . . . . . . . 172
                        women . . . . . . . . 160
                        men  . . . . . . . . . 12
            Classification . . . . . . . . . . . . . . . . . . . .  28
                        women . . . . . . . . 27
                        men  . . . . . . . . .  1
            Exclusion . . . . . . . . . . . . . . . . . . . . . . .  8
                                (all female)

Employment Agency Practices (all female)  . . . . . . . . . . . . . . .  13
            Testing  . . . . . . . . . . . . . . . . . . . . .  1
            Referral . . . . . . . . . . . . . . . . . . . . . 10
            Classification . . . . . . . . . . . . . . . . . .  2

Labor-Management Practices (all female)  . . . . . . . . . . . . . . . .  3
            Training/Retraining . . . . . . . . . . . . . . .  2
            Discrimination . . . . . . . . . . . . . . . . . .  1

Employer-Union-Agency Practices (all female) . . . . . . . . . . . . . .  96
            Advertising . . . . . . . . . . . . . . . . . . . 94
            Retaliation . . . . . . . . . . . . . . . . . . .  2

Unspecified Respondent (all female) . . . . . . . . . . . . . . . . . . .  9
            Discharge . . . . . . . . . . . . . . . . . . . .  2
            Compensation  . . . . . . . . . . . . . . . . . .  3
            Terms . . . . . . . . . . . . . . . . . . . . . .  2
            Classification . . . . . . . . . . . . . . . . . .  2
```

SOURCE: Equal Employment Opportunity Commission, *Second Annual Report*, 1966-1967.

Table XII

CLASSIFICATION OF SEX DISCRIMINATION COMPLAINTS
RECEIVED BY THE EQUAL EMPLOYMENT OPPORTUNITY
COMMISSION DURING THIRD YEAR OF OPERATION
1967-1968

Total Sex Discrimination Charges			2,410
Employer Practices			2,072
Hiring		208	
	women 160		
	men 48		
Discharge		207	
	women 199		
	men 8		
Compensation		398	
	women 388		
	men 10		
Terms		964	
	women 868		
	men 96		
Conditions		130	
	women 110		
	men 20		
Classification		118	
	women 111		
	men 7		
Miscellaneous		47	
	women 42		
	men 5		
Union Practices			300
Exclusion		18	
	women 18		
	men 0		
Discrimination		241	
	women 204		
	men 37		
Classification		41	
	women 41		
	men 6		
Employer Agency Practices			20
Referral		14	
	women 8		
	men 6		
Testing		6	
	women 5		
	men 1		
Labor-Management			1
Training/Retraining			

continued

49

Table XII
(continued)

Employer-Union-Agency Practices 17
          Retaliation 7
                    women 7
                    men 0
          Advertising 10
                    women 8
                    men 2

SOURCE: Equal Employment Opportunity Commission, *Third Annual Report,*
1967-1968.

investigation, deferred for state or local action, or returned for
additional information. Of these, 2 689 pertained to sex. The Equal
Employment Opportunity Commission's statistical breakdown in
its Fourth Annual Report shows the year's charges based on sex
as follows:

Total complaints received 17,272
Sex discrimination complaints 2,689
Recommended for investigation 1,922
Deferred for state or local FEPC action 268
Additional information required 501

1969-1970
Sex discrimination complaints in 1969-1970 were 3,597 out of
17,903 charges either recommended for investigation, deferred for
state or local FEPC action, or returned for additional information.
A statistical analysis, based on the Fifth Annual Report of the
Equal Employment Opportunity Commission, shows:

Total complaints received 20,122
Sex discrimination complaints 3,597
Recommended for investigation 2,370
Deferred for state or local FEPC action 406
Additional information required 413

Although the number of complaints increased substantially from
2,689 in 1969 to 3,597 in 1970, the percent of discrimination charges
based on sex remains about 20 percent. The percentage consis-
tency is due to corresponding increases in complaints based on
race. The Equal Opportunity Commission estimates sex discrimination complaints during 1971 to number 4,500; racial complaints
15,000; and total discrimination charges, which include race, sex,
religion, and national origin, to total 22,000+.

Of the discrimination charges received for which there is no probable jurisdiction, 399 pertained to sex, as follows:

Untimely. 246
Less than 50 employers 2
Political subdivision 29
Educational institution. 2
U. S. Government 26
Not covered by Title VII. 94

Commission Rulings

The most common problems the Equal Employment Opportunity Commission has encountered as it attempts to end job discrimination include: (a) job classification, (b) seniority lines and wage rates, (c) state protective legislation, (d) classified advertising, (e) insurance, (f) married and pregnant women, (g) discharge, (h) referral by employment agencies, (i) hire, (j) promotion, (d) promotion, (k) retirement age, and (l) pension benefits.

Job classification

The Commission has stated, as a general rule, maintenance of separate jobs for men and women is unlawful, unless sex is termed a "bona fide occupational qualification" for the job (for example, female models for female clothing). Otherwise, employers violate Title VII when they exclude women from jobs.

Even weightlifting standards cannot be set on the basis of sex. These standards require consideration of all relevant factors, such as physical ability of the individual involved, type materials to be lifted or carried, the height or distance material is to be lifted or carried, and the frequency of lifting or carrying.[5] Each case must be decided on an individual basis. However, state laws and regulations that are still protective of the woman worker are considered bona fide occupational qualifications. Weightlifting regulations usually will be honored except where pounds are unreasonably low. A company policy prohibiting women from employment on jobs requiring lifting or carrying more than 35 pounds was found lawful.[6]

Another Commission ruling in the area of bona fide occupational qualifications concerns the airlines' position of flight cabin attendant. The airlines contended that because of desired feminine qualities in flight cabin attendants, only women could fill the position. The Commission ruled:

When a job is involved which both men and women are able to perform satisfactorily, employers may not lawfully restrict that job to members of one sex because of their assumptions about the personality characteristics of men or women as a class.[7]

Sex is not a bona fide occupational qualification for the position of flight cabin attendant, and an airline which pursues a policy of employing only females as flight attendants violates Title VII.

A noteworthy case is *Clarence H. Hailes* v. *Pan American World Airways, Inc.,* in which the plaintiff alleges he applied for a position as a flight cabin attendant and was denied an interview because he is a male. The respondent contends sex is a bona fide occupational qualification for its position of flight cabin attendant.

Classified advertising

Advertisers may not specify "male" or "female" in help-wanted advertising unless sex is a bona fide occupational qualification for the job. The Equal Employment Opportunity Commission issued a guideline in August, 1968, effective December 1, 1968, indicating placement of ads in columns headed "Help-Wanted, Male" and "Help-Wanted, Female" would constitute a violation of Title VII unless sex were a bona fide occupational qualification for the job involved.

In December, 1968, the *New York Times* changed its classified advertising format to comply with this guideline. American Newspaper Publishers Association and the *Washington Evening Star,* however, brought suit in the local district court requesting the Commission's ruling be declared invalid. The effective date of the guideline was stayed by an Order of the United States District Court for the District of Columbia in November, 1968; on January 24, 1969, the United States Court of Appeals for the District of Columbia issued an Order vacating the Stay granted by the District Court.

The United States Equal Employment Opportunity Commission's guideline concerning sex discrimination in job advertising, delayed by court action, was in effect as of January 24, 1969, and it provides:

It is a violation of Title VII for a help wanted advertisement to indicate a preference, limitation, specification, or discrimination based on sex unless sex is a bona fide occupational qualification for the particular job involved. The placement of an advertisement in columns classified by publishers on the basis of sex, such as columns headed "Male" or "Female" will be considered an expression of a preference, limitation, specification, or discrimination based on sex.[8]

State protective legislation

Many states have laws which limit the type of jobs women may hold, hours they may work, and which, in general, prescribe certain conditions of employment for women, such as minimum and overtime pay, seating and restroom facilities, and lunch and rest periods. Many of these state labor laws for women, no longer relevant under twentieth century working conditions, conflict with Title VII.

Prior to February 1967 the Commission had not decided cases which conflicted with state law. The Commission had referred these cases to the civil courts. In February 1968 the Commission issued guidelines stating it would decide, on an individual basis, whether the laws actually protected the women from hazards or had the effect of discriminating against them. Specifically, the Commission stated, "...where the effect of state protective legislations appears to be discriminatory rather than protective, the Commission will proceed to decide whether that legislation is superseded by the Act."

Significant changes in state protective labor legislation. Although much civil litigation has resulted from the conflicts between Title VII and individual state labor laws, many states were motivated by Title VII to modify or repeal various sex discriminatory protective laws. For example, significant changes in state protective labor legislation in 1966 and 1967 occurred in the following states:

Delaware, in 1965, repealed its hours laws.

Michigan, in 1967, repealed its hours laws and a law prohibiting women from operating or using certain wheels and belts.

Pennsylvania, in 1966, amended its hours law to give the Commissioner of Labor power to grant exemptions to permit women to work overtime, providing such work is voluntary and paid at least time and one half the regular rate of pay.

Virginia, in 1966, amended its hours law to exempt firms which meet the wage, hours, overtime, and recordkeeping requirements of the Fair Labor Standards Act.

North Carolina, in 1967, exempted women subject to the Fair Labor Standards Act from its law restricting women to 9 hours a day and 48 hours a week. Such women remain subject to a 10-hour-a-day, 55-hour-a-week law and a 11-hour-a-day, 55-hour-a-week law, both of which apply to small establishments.

California, in 1967, amended its hours law to permit women covered by the FLSA, with some industry exceptions, to work up to 10 hours a day and 58 hours a week, providing they receive premium overtime pay after 8 hours a day and 40 hours a week.

Maryland, in 1967, amended its hours law to exempt women covered under bona fide collective bargaining agreements and repealed its night work laws.

Oregon, in 1967, repealed its maximum hours law, but permits the Wage and Hour Commission to set maximum hours for women under the minimum wage program. However, women subject to the Federal Fair Labor Standards Act are excluded from this program.

Nebraska, amended its hours law to permit women to work up to 12 hours a day and 60 a week on permit of the Labor Commissioner and if overtime is voluntary.

The District of Columbia, in 1966, exempted executive, professional, and administrative employees.

Massachusetts, in 1966, exempted executive, professional, and administrative personnel.

Colorado, in 1967, exempted women in a bona fide executive, administrative, professional, or clerical capacity.

Illinois, in 1967, exempted women in professional, executive, and administrative positions earning more than $100 per week. Assistants to those in professional, executive, and administrative positions are excepted.

Arizona, in 1966, amended its law to permit women and girls to work, in an emergency, up to 10 hours daily but not more than 48 hours a week, and to require that at least one and one-half times the regular rate be paid for hours over 8 in a day.

New York, in 1965, extended until July 1, 1968, the law permitting females and minors dispensation from certain legal re-

54

quirements as to hours and other conditions when a defense emergency exists. Previously this law had been extended on a year-to-year basis. Several other minor changes were made in 1966 and 1967.

Seniority policies and wage rates

The Commission stated that as a general rule seniority policies based on sex are unlawful. Where discriminatory seniority systems have been maintained, it may be necessary to merge and provide for open bidding between seniority lines or to make adjustments in seniority standing of current employees. A related subject is discriminatory wage rates. Sometimes wage rates of certain jobs are undervalued because such jobs were always held by women. Where this can be established, such wage rates must be re-evaluated and corrected.

Married and pregnant women

The Equal Employment Opportunity Commission has ruled an employer may not refuse to hire married women, nor can female employees be discharged when they marry unless a similar rule applies to males. As a general rule, an employer may not terminate a female employee for pregnancy without offering her a leave of absence with the right to return to the same or an equivalent job. Where this may not be possible, the employer may be justified in offering the employee another job or preferential consideration for future openings. The Commission has also said that an employer's requirement that pregnant females take a ninety-day leave prior to delivery is not unreasonable; and that in most instances a five or six months' maternity leave should be adequate.[9]

Sylvia Porter in her syndicated column, commented that prior to the passage of Title VII, pregnant employees in

> 56.8 percent of the offices and 26.3 percent of the plants surveyed are asked to resign—although some of the firms will retroactively consider the employee to have been on leave if she returns to work within, say, a year and if she remains at least another year or two.
>
> A full four out of five companies set a cut-off date for working, even though the woman had medical authorization to work longer. While some ask her to stop at three or four months, a more frequent cut-off is six months.[10]

The airlines industry has been active in litigation involving marriage of stewardesses. The airlines contended that employment of married stewardesses would lead to operational and administrative problems as well as cause marital difficulties for stewardesses. The Commission ruled that termination of stewardesses on marriage is a sex-based condition of employment. Various airlines employ male flight attendants, and no policy of termination on marriage was or is applied to them. Therefore, the requirement of single status is not related to satisfactory performance as a flight attendant but to identity of the attendant. The irrelevance of marriage to satisfactory job performance of flight attendants is further demonstrated, the Commission ruled, by the fact that the no-marriage ban is not even uniformly applied to female flight attendants throughout the airlines industry. Thus, no-marriage restrictions on stewardesses is in violation of Title VII.[11]

Retirement age and pension benefits

In February, 1968, the Commission issued guidelines stating that employers must offer male and female employees equal privileges with regard to optional and compulsory retirement ages, and that it would begin processing charges involving such differences July, 1968.

Further, the Commission would decide other sex-based differences in pension plans, such as survivor benefits, on an individual case basis. Specifically, the guidelines state:

(a) A difference in optional or compulsory retirement ages based on sex violates Title VII.

(b) Other differences based on sex, such as differences in benefits for survivors, will be decided by the Commission by the issuance of Commission decisions in cases raising such issues.

Insurance benefits

The Equal Employment Opportunity Commission has made these insurance pronouncements: An employer must either make equal medical, hospital, accident, and life insurance benefits available to men and women, or must make equal contributions toward such benefits. Where companies provide maternity benefits for the wives of male employees, they must provide such benefits for female employees. Where companies provide coverage, such as accident coverage, for the wives and families of male employees, they must make similar coverage available for the husbands and families of female employees.

Sex Discrimination at the Management Level

As shown by statistical information presented in this chapter, sex discrimination is a major area of complaint. However, discrimination complaints in terms of sex for management-level employees have been so insignificant that the Equal Employment Opportunity Commission does not maintain a special reporting category.

Not many women in management, then, formally complain of discrimination in preventing them from moving to higher levels or for receiving lesser compensation than their male colleagues. Several reasons for this can be offered:

1. *Women account for a small percentage of all management personnel.* Logically, discrimination complaints from women in management could not comprise too large a proportion of all sex discrimination complaints.

2. *Discrimination at the management level may be much more subtle than at the lower levels within an organization.* While written criteria exist (wage rates, seniority policies, overtime practices, clear-cut union classifications) at the operative levels, job requirements at higher levels become more intangible. No objective, evaluative measures exist against which the fairness of management's employment practices and policies can be compared.

Thus, within the management hierarchy a woman may not be considered for advancement for subjective and prejudicial reasons. But to assert and sufficiently prove such discrimination in a civil suit is apparently very difficult. Many women have complained that top management has often encouraged them to seek higher positions but neutralize these proddings by never finding the "right" woman with the "right" qualifications for the job.

3. *Women may be reluctant to put their jobs on the line by filing a discrimination charge.* Statistics on why women work show economics motivates most women. Individuals dependent upon their jobs are hesitant to threaten this economic livelihood. Espousing sex discrimination, no matter how legitimate the complaint, jeopardizes future possibilities that may arise. A woman may hesitate to risk everything for what she feels would probably be a futile fight anyway.

4. *Many individuals at the professional level may feel sex discrimination litigation is unprofessional and conflicts with their professional ethics.*

5. *Women's aspiration levels appear to some observers to be lower than men's.* Women's dual role perhaps tempers their concentrated efforts in career spheres and tends to lower their willingness to assume executive responsibilities and demands. Traditionally, most women appear to find their greatest need-gratification from marriage and family.

6. *Women may not be expected to pursue a career, and to be a manager or supervisor has been viewed as unfeminine.* Women who have crossed the management lines have been branded in some instances as more "masculine" and "aggressive" than feminine. To some extent, it has not been "becoming" for a "lady" to work as a manager or supervisor. Some women do not desire to challenge this social image.

7. *Some women have accepted psychologically a secondary role in the business world without major complaint.* These women apparently think of themselves as secretaries, or as administrative assistants. Among themselves, they appear to feel unqualified and incompetent to handle the intrigues of directing business actions. They lack confidence in their business capabilities.

The following comments from acknowledged expert observers explain the rationale in support of the above explanations.

Equal Employment Opportunity Commission's senior attorney, Sonia Pressman, speculates in a recent letter:

> It is my understanding that few charges to date have been filed by professional men or women; this may be because such individuals work for employers of 25 or fewer employees; because discrimination involving the refusal to hire or to promote professional individuals is more difficult to establish than discrimination involving individuals engaged in blue collar and clerical work; or because professional individuals do not tend to make complaints of discrimination to state and federal agencies.[12]

In an address to the Business and Professional Women's Club, Miss Pressman, in discussing why women have filed so few charges, even though the exclusion of women from the "executive suite" is traditional, said:

> It may be because professional employees are frequently employed by smaller companies which have only recently been

covered by Title VII or are still not within the Act's jurisdiction; because discrimination involving the refusal to hire or promote professional employees is more difficult to establish than that involving individuals engaged in blue-collar and clerical work because determinations as to job qualifications are less quantifiable; because professional employees are often unorganized and thus do not have the assistance of labor unions in processing complaints of discrimination; because executive and professional employees have a closer working relationship with their superiors and thus a greater fear of the effect that filing charges may have on that relationship; and because professional employees do not tend to make complaints of discrimination to federal agencies.[13]

Marilyn Mercer, in her study of women at work, "Is There Room at the Top?" observed:

Although one third of all complaints registered with the Equal Employment Opportunity Commission have charged discrimination because of sex, the vast majority of these concern pay and promotions at the blue-collar level, where clear-cut union classifications protect the complainant. . . . White-collar women, with no union behind them are not usually anxious to make these kinds of waves.[14]

What to Expect in the Seventies

Unless lack of executives in the 1970's (from an expected shortage of middle-aged men) and increased emphasis for quality personnel force business to utilize more women, the volume of sex complaints at management levels may increase in the seventies.

Women are formally organizing their efforts to change the second-class status of American women. A priority goal of these various influential groups is to help women advance in management.

Influential organizations actively supporting Title VII

These groups of organized women seem to stem from two origins: a much older movement which dates back to the suffragettes, and a recent movement of young women, perhaps an offshoot of the youth movement, often called the "women's liberation movement."

National Women's Party. National Women's Party, the senior organization of these groups, is an outgrowth of the Congressional Union for Women's Suffrage. Its counterpart, the National American

Woman's Suffrage Association, after the Nineteenth Amendment (1920), emerged into the League for Women Voters. The National Women's Party is concerned with "equality of rights under the law."

Governmental organizations. In addition to encouraging women to seek more ambitious positions and continue their education, many of these groups attempt to influence federal and state governments with regard to more effective utilization of women in our society. In 1920 the Women's Bureau in the Department of Labor was established with enhancement of employed women's status as its prime objective. Recently, another organization, Federally Employed Women (FEW) has been formed not only to enhance the status of women in government service, but to help recruit capable women for employment. FEW consists of women who have received the Federal Woman's Award for outstanding federal service. Also, the President's Commission on the Status of Women was created in 1961, and subsequently resulted in fifty state commissions on the status of women.

National Organization for Women (NOW). National Organization for Women, formed in 1966 to stimulate action *now* for American women, promotes the social and professional status of women. The following legislative program illustrates the range of NOW's goals:

I. EQUAL RIGHTS AMENDMENT

II. EQUAL OPPORTUNITY IN EDUCATION

(a) There should be no discrimination on the basis of sex in schools that receive federal funds.

(b) Award of scholarship, fellowship and other benefits should be made without regard to sex.

III. EQUAL OPPORTUNITY IN EMPLOYMENT

(a) Enforcement of Title VII (Civil Rights Act of 1964).

(b) Enforcement of federal contract compliance.

(c) Equal treatment for women in federal training and job opportunity programs, such as OEO, MDTA, and Vocational Education Act.

(d) Extension of Fair Labor Standards Act and Equal Pay Act to cover all workers.

(e) Child Care Facilities for Working Parents.

(f) Protection of Employment Rights during Maternity. Women should receive maternity leave as a form of social security and/or employee benefit (similar to sick leave or job security because of the draft for men). Women must be ensured the right to return to their jobs within a reasonable time after childbirth, without loss of seniority or other accrued benefits.

IV. REPEAL OF ABORTION LAWS

V. REVIEW OF INCOME TAX LAWS, SOCIAL SECURITY LAWS AND RETIREMENT PLANS

(a) Eliminate tax provisions that discriminate against single persons.

(b) Allow deductions for child care, whether or not child may be listed as dependent.

(c) Social security laws should be revised to eliminate discrimination against working wives.

(d) Social security laws should be revised to eliminate discrimination against divorced women.

(e) Retirement and pension plans should be revised to eliminate discrimination on the basis of sex.

VI. IDENTIFYING AND REPORTING ON SEX DISCRIMINATION

Agencies should be established on all governmental levels to investigate, study and report on sex discrimination in all areas of life. The Conference supports Congresswoman Griffiths' bill to broaden the Civil Rights Commission mandate of studying and reporting on discrimination based on race, color, religion or national origin to include sex.

VIII. INCLUDING WOMEN IN APPOINTIVE POSITIONS IN GOVERNMENT

There should be legislation to include women on all commissions, boards and other appointive bodies at all governmental levels.

Women's liberation movement. While all past efforts are instrumental in bringing women so far, perhaps the most dramatic impetus is yet to come, and from a new feminist movement. This

61

movement, seemingly synonymous with the youth movement, has infiltrated the college campus, the city scene; everywhere, young women voice adamant objections to society's entire sexist structure and usually with the support of such newly founded organizations as Women's Equity Action League (WEAL), Women's Radical Action Project (WRAP), Women's International Terrorist Conspiracy from Hell (WITCH), Redstockings, Union for Women's International Liberation (UWIL), Female Liberation, Women's Liberation Front, or Radical Women.

These young militants heap pressure as never before on business and society to erase sexism. Less intimidated, more aware, and with more courage and conviction to express and act on their views than any previous female generation, they say they are willing to put everything on the line to change traditional concepts of what women can and cannot, should and should not, do.

It is not a question of ability anymore; women have proved they can make it in competitive business if given a fair chance. And growing numbers of businessmen are optimistic industry will soon compete for women in the job marketplace in the same way it does for men. They feel management practices in the seventies will radically change to reflect economic forces, new technology, and 1970 social attitudes. But, if they don't, these young women, unwilling to sit idly by and accept second-class status without protest, are determined to make the changes themselves. Perhaps they have learned from history that usually if all hell isn't raised, very little change occurs.

Perhaps the question is: Are men ready to accept women among their executive ranks on these terms? And if not, what happens?

Chapter VI

EXECUTIVES' OPINIONS OF WOMEN IN MANAGEMENT

Lyrics to a popular commercial say, "You've come a long way, baby," but many women add, "We've still a long way to go." Some experienced observers feel that the new movement of dissatisfied females is fast surging into a revolution. Until recently, women suffered discrimination in silence; they said little, complained little, and wrote little about how they really feel. But women no longer choose to suffer what they feel is exploitation in the job marketplace. To illustrate, a recent brochure announcing a national caucus for professional women said, in part: "Victor Hugo's statement, 'No army can withstand the force of an idea whose time has come' appears to express the new activism, even militancy, of women this year. It is time for an end to second class citizenship for women."

The momentum builds as mountains of pamphlets circulate, as women join forces in newly created organizations, as newspaper and magazine articles hit by the number, as conferences, seminars, caucuses are held everyday—all to report protests of women over their sex and economic exploitation. Much more serious than it first appears, these are warnings for society to take a realistic, "like-it-is" look at women.

How do men really feel about women in executive ranks? Do business and service professions, in competition for well-educated, highly motivated executives, overlook their most obvious resource, women? To what degree does discrimination, in fact, exist against women in management?

To learn some of the contemporary attitudes and business practices toward women, 900 business executives throughout the United States were surveyed: 300 from large corporations, 300 from small corporations, and 300 women in management positions. The need for the study is predicated on the assumption that our society needs the fullest possible economic contribution from all working citizens regardless of age, color, or sex. Hopefully, it will help point the way to more effective utilization of women in management. Further, this investigation may help in policy formulation by government and private industry, as well as serve as a guide to future legislation. Definitely, it should provide additional insight to women interested in a career at the top executive levels. Below is a capsule summary of these survey findings.[1]

Employment

All respondees, big businesses, small businesses, and women in management, were asked the question, "What percent of management personnel in your organization are women?" As shown in Table XIII, 31 percent of big businesses' respondees, 43.7 percent of small business respondees, and 33.3 percent of women in management reported that less than 2 percent of their management personnel are women. In each survey category, well over 50 percent of all respondees reported less than 5 percent of management personnel are women. Small businesses apparently have fewer women employed in management percentage-wise than big businesses. The women-in-management category, which represented all sizes of businesses, responded in approximately the same manner.

Other studies[2] have indicated that women account for only 2 percent of all management personnel. This study suggests that the 2 percent figure may be low. It can be noted that between 6 and 9

Table XIII

EXTENT TO WHICH WOMEN ARE EMPLOYED AT
MANAGEMENT LEVEL AMONG RESPONDEES

Percent of Management Personnel Who Are Women	Respondee Classification					
	Big Businesses		Small Businesses		Women in Management	
	N	%	N	%	N	%
0-2	25	31	28	43.7	50	33.3
3-5	20	24	14	21.9	32	22.4
6-10	15	19	11	16.9	20	13.9
11-15	10	12	6	8.7	15	11.0
16-25	7	9	3	6.3	9	6.3
26-40	3	4	1	2.5	10	7.5
41-Over	1	1	0	0	8	5.6

SOURCE: Survey conducted among selected sample of big businesses, small businesses, and women in management.

percent of the companies responding had between 16 and 25 percent of management personnel as women. Approximately one third of all respondees had 2 percent or less women in management. Between 20 and 25 percent had 3 to 5 percent of their management force as women. Companies employing the largest number of women in management were banks, insurance companies, and merchandising firms.

Level of Responsibility

As shown in Table XIV, all the companies responding for both big and small businesses indicated that, of all their female management personnel, only 2 percent or less were employed at the senior level. Women have made their greatest penetration into management at the middle and first levels. Clearly, few women in responding companies employed as management personnel have advanced to the policy-making level. Among the responding companies that had a relatively large percent of women employed at the lower level were banks, insurance companies, and transportation companies (primarily airlines).

Women-in-management were not asked the question regarding level of responsibility.

Table XIV

DISTRIBUTION OF WOMEN IN MANAGEMENT ACCORDING
TO LEVEL OF RESPONSIBILITY*

Management Level % Range	Respondee Classification											
	Big Businesses						Small Businesses					
	Senior		Middle		First Level		Senior		Middle		First Level	
	N	%	N	%	N	%	N	%	N	%	N	%
0-2	81	100	0	0	0	0	63	100	0	0	0	0
3-5	0	0	11	13.6	0	0	0	0	20	31.7	0	0
6-10	0	0	30	37.0	11	13.6	0	0	23	36.5	14	22.2
11-15	0	0	30	37.0	20	24.7	0	0	10	15.9	25	39.7
16-25	0	0	10	12.4	40	49.3	0	0	10	15.9	15	23.8
25-Over	0	0	0	0	10	12.4	0	0	0	0	9	14.3

SOURCE: Survey conducted among selected sample of big businesses and small businesses.
*For example, 30 (or 37 percent) of the big business firms reported that 6-10 percent of their women in managerial positions were at the middle level of management.

Although few or no women were employed at senior levels within the responding companies, one company had this to say:

The company now has five women who are officers of the company, although not at the senior level. All of them have been elected since 1964. For a great many years we have had a rather large number of women in the first level of management. The women who are presently officers are line officers, except for one who serves in a staff capacity. We have felt that we are making very substantial progress in the matter of expanding opportunities for women in management jobs, and, certainly, we are very well satisfied with those that we have in such capacities. We believe that many more women than formerly are interested in management positions. I think generally that the men in our company have been very glad to see women recognized for their achievements and have applauded their advance into officer status.

Another company (a public utility) said:

Some 13% of all the women employed by the 21 Telephone Operating Companies are in management. Of our total management force 47% are women. In looking at growth in management jobs held by women since 1964, our figures indicate an overall increase of 36%. Of special interest is the increase of women in management jobs above the first level of management. This increase is about 53%.

Another company (insurance) was not as optimistic as the previous companies, though it was encouraging regarding women's advance to senior levels in management:

Because of the general nature of our office jobs and the traditions of our society, we employ, as you might expect, a very large number of women in our Home Office operations. Many have advanced to positions of supervisory and management responsibility. I do not wish to imply, however, that we are entirely satisfied with the number we have been able to attract and hold in management positions.

The brightest spot that I see in improving our position is that we have been highly successful recently in employing women college graduates. They have been placed in a variety of advanced technical positions from which they will have excel-

66

lent opportunity to move into management. Last year, for example, we hired 340 college graduates of whom 133, or 39%, were women. This represents an increase over the number we were able to hire several years ago. We follow a policy of promoting people to management from within the organization. If we can continue to hire significant numbers of top quality women college graduates, we will be able to move more of them into management positions in the future.

Line Management Positions

Respondees were asked the question, "How has the percent of line management positions filled by women changed since the enactment of Title VII in 1964?"

Of big business respondees, 3.4 percent reported a decrease in utilization of women in line management positions since enactment of Title VII in 1964. Meanwhile, 25.9 percent of the women in management, who in many if not most cases did not have access to actual employment information, reported a decrease in utilization of women in management. Since big businesses and small businesses reported little decline, it is probable that the estimate from women indicates an element of emotion which is not supported by factual data.

Over 60 percent of all respondees reported no change in utilization of women in line management capacities since enactment of Title VII.

A considerable percentage, 31.7 percent of the small businesses and 26.3 percent of the big businesses, reported an increase in utilization of women in line capacities (Table XV). It cannot be determined, however, from these data whether enactment of Title VII is responsible for the reported increase. Only 6.4 percent of the women in management reported an increase, again perhaps suggesting certain subjectivity.

Staff Management Positions

Data presented in Table XVI indicate that the utilization of women in staff capacities since 1964 has followed the same general pattern as utilization of women in line capacities. Again, women in management seem to reflect more pessimism about what has happened, with 18.6 percent believing that there has been an actual decrease in employment of women in staff management and only 8 percent of the women in management feeling there has been an

Table XV

CHANGE IN UTILIZATION OF WOMEN IN
LINE MANAGEMENT POSITIONS SINCE
ENACTMENT OF TITLE VII IN 1964

Degree of Change	Big Businesses		Respondee Classification Small Businesses		Women in Management	
	N	%	N	%	N	%
Decrease	3	3.4	0	0	37	25.9
No Change	49	60.5	40	63.5	92	63.3
Increase	21	26.3	20	31.7	9	6.4
No Reply	8	9.8	3	4.8	6	4.4

SOURCE: Survey conducted among selected sample of big businesses, small businesses, and women in management.

Table XVI

CHANGE IN UTILIZATION OF WOMEN EMPLOYED IN
STAFF MANAGEMENT POSITIONS SINCE ENACTMENT
OF TITLE VII IN 1964

Degree of Change	Big Businesses		Respondee Classification Small Businesses		Women in Management	
	N	%	N	%	N	%
Decrease	4	4.9	0	0	27	18.6
No Change	55	67.9	39	61.4	103	71.3
Increase	13	16.1	18	28.0	11	8.0
No Reply	9	11.1	6	10.6	3	2.1

SOURCE: Survey conducted among selected sample of big businesses, small businesses, and women in management.

increase. Significantly, well over 60 percent of all respondees report there has been no change since 1964. However, it is noteworthy that 16.1 percent of the big businesses and 28 percent of small businesses indicated an increase.

Emotional Factors

An effort was made to determine whether any differences exist among respondees relative to emotional factors of women in management when compared with men. As shown in Table XVII, a substantial percentage of women in management (75 percent) felt women are more intuitive than men, while 46.9 percent of big business respondees felt no difference exists. Meanwhile, small business respondees were more inclined than big business respondees to think that women are more intuitive than men.

Big business respondees visualize women as being more emotional than men.

When asked "Are women more intelligent?" 43.6 percent of the women in management respondees replied "yes." Big business respondees were the most conservative with only 17.3 percent answering "yes," while approximately one third of all small businesses answered "yes." Significantly, two thirds of big business respondees said "There is no difference."

"Are women in management more ambitious than men?" A substantial majority (70.4 percent) of big business respondees said, "no difference." However, only 17.5 percent of the small businesses said "no difference;" and, 38.1 percent of the women in management respondees said "no difference."

Women in management viewed themselves as being more logical than men, as compared with big business and small business respondees. Big businesses, to a larger extent than either small businesses or women in management respondees, said there is no difference in the degree of logic of women in management when compared with men.

In terms of dedication, women visualized themselves as being much more dedicated than men, as compared with big business and small business respondees. Over 60 percent of the small business respondees saw no difference in the degree of dedication of women when compared with men in management.

Areas of Responsibility

Respondees were asked, "What percent of management personnel (line and staff) in each of the functional areas stated below (accounting, finance, sales, production, data processing, administrative, other) is female?"

As shown in Table XVIII, women have made their greatest penetration into management in big businesses in general administration, data processing, accounting, and production. Meanwhile, in small businesses women are shown to hold greatest penetration in production, followed by administration, accounting, and sales.

Table XVII

VIEWPOINT OF RESPONDEES TOWARD EMOTIONAL FACTORS OF WOMEN IN MANAGEMENT WHEN COMPARED WITH MEN
(Data shown as average percentage for responding companies)

	Respondee Classification																
	YES						NO						NO DIFFERENCE					
When Compared With Men Are Women More:	Big Businesses		Small Businesses		Women in Management		Big Businesses		Small Businesses		Women in Management		Big Businesses		Small Businesses		Women in Management	
	N	%	N	%	N	%	N	%	N	%	N	%	N	%	N	%	N	%
Intuitive	7	8.7	14	22.2	108	75.0	36	44.4	23	36.5	12	8.4	38	46.9	26	41.3	24	16.6
Emotional	60	74.0	33	52.4	84	58.3	14	17.3	17	27.0	28	19.4	7	8.7	13	20.6	32	27.3
Intelligent	14	17.3	21	33.3	63	43.6	15	18.5	12	19.0	1	.4	52	64.2	30	47.7	80	56.0
Ambitious	15	17.3	8	12.0	42	29.2	10	12.3	44	70.5	47	32.7	56	70.4	11	17.5	55	38.1
Logical	6	7.4	5	8.4	24	16.7	34	42.0	28	44.4	52	46.1	41	50.6	30	47.6	68	37.2
Dedicated	32	39.5	16	26.0	78	54.2	11	14.6	8	12.2	15	10.4	38	45.9	39	61.8	51	35.4

SOURCE: Survey conducted among selected sample of big businesses, small businesses, and women in management.

Table XVIII

FUNCTIONAL AREAS IN WHICH LARGEST PERCENT OF WOMEN
ARE EMPLOYED IN RESPONDING COMPANIES*

| | Respondee Classification | | | |
| | Big Businesses | | Small Businesses | |
Functional Area	N	%	N	%
Accounting	11	13.6	9	14.3
Finance	2	2.5	1	1.6
Sales	9	11.1	6	9.5
Production	15	18.5	22	34.9
Data Processing	17	20.9	2	3.2
Administrative	24	29.7	21	33.3
Other	3	3.7	2	3.2

SOURCE: Survey conducted among selected sample of big businesses and small businesses.

*For example, 11, or 13.6 percent, of the large firms have a greater number of women in accounting than in other areas.

Significantly, in big businesses women were much more important numerically in terms of management in the sales function as compared with small businesses.

Women did not appear to have made any substantial penetration into management in the finance function of business.

Small businesses, to a considerable degree, were more apt to place women in management positions in performance of the production than were big businesses.

Because women in management were not expected to have access to actual employment figures, they were not asked this question.

Past Experience

As shown in Table XIX, responding companies were asked to select one statement which best described their experience in using women at the management level. Only a small percent of respondees in both big businesses and small businesses described their experience with women in management as "excellent." A majority (58 percent) of big businesses described their experience as "very good," while 30 percent of small businesses described

Table XIX

EXPERIENCE OF RESPONDEE COMPANIES IN UTILIZATION OF WOMEN IN MANAGEMENT

Statement Describing Experience	Big Businesses		Small Businesses	
	N	%	N	%
"Excellent. Women in general perform very well in management, often better than men."	2	2.5	4	6.3
"Very good. Women do a fine job—equal to men."	47	58.0	19	30.2
"Good. No real problems or complaints."	22	27.1	23	36.6
"Poor. Women just don't adjust to responsibilities of management."	4	4.9	12	19.0
Companies not responding to this question.	6	7.5	5	7.9

SOURCE: Survey conducted among selected sample of big businesses and small businesses.

their experience as "very good." Twenty-seven percent, significantly, of the big businesses and 36 percent of the small businesses described their experience as "good." Only a small percent of big businesses (4.9 percent) described their experience as "poor," but a significant portion (19 percent) of small businesses rated their experience as poor. Nothing was learned in the survey to indicate why so many more small businesses have had disappointing results in using women in management than big businesses.

It can be concluded from the data that most respondees were satisfied with the performance of women in management.

Women's Interest in Management Positions

An effort was made to determine whether enactment of Title VII in 1964 stimulated more women to seek management level jobs. Only 7.4 percent of big businesses and 4.8 percent of small businesses responding said that "Many more women are seeking management jobs." The "More, but not substantially so" category was indicated by almost 30 percent of the big businesses but by only 12.7 percent of the small businesses. (See Table XX.)

Table XX

CHANGE IN DEGREE OF INTEREST AMONG WOMEN SEEKING
MANAGEMENT POSITIONS SINCE ENACTMENT OF TITLE VII

| Degree of Change | Respondee Classification | | | |
| | Big Businesses | | Small Businesses | |
	N	%	N	%
Many more women are seeking management jobs.	6	7.4	3	4.8
More but not substantially so.	24	29.6	8	12.7
No noticeable difference.	44	54.3	43	68.3
Actually, women seem to be less interested in seeking management jobs than before.	2	2.5	3	4.7
Companies not responding.	5	6.2	6	9.5

SOURCE: Survey conducted among selected sample of big businesses and small businesses.

The most significant fact developed from this question was that there is "no noticeable difference," which was indicated by 54.3 percent of the big businesses and 68.3 percent of the small businesses. A very small number of the responding companies actually indicated that there are fewer women seeking management jobs than before enactment of Title VII.

It appears, then, that Title VII has had only a token effect on the interest of women to move into management-level jobs.

Discrimination

All three categories of respondees were asked the question, "Not considering only your own company but American business in general, do you feel women are discriminated against in management?" (Table XXI).

Almost half of the big business respondees (49.4 percent) and 76 percent of small business respondees said "yes." Women in management by a substantial majority (70 percent) also agreed that dis-

73

Table XXI

VIEWS OF RESPONDEES TOWARD QUESTION "DOES DISCRIMINATION
AGAINST WOMEN IN MANAGEMENT IN FACT EXIST?"

| | Respondee Classification | | | | | |
| Response | Big Businesses | | Small Businesses | | Women in Management | |
	N	%	N	%	N	%
Yes	40	49.4	48	76.2	101	70.2
No	24	29.7	6	9.5	39	27.1
No answer	17	20.9	9	14.3	4	2.7

SOURCE: Survey conducted among selected sample of big businesses, small businesses, and women in management.

crimination does, in fact, exist. A significant percent of both big and small businesses did not respond to this question, perhaps indicating some uncertainty on this subjective question.

Those respondees who answered the discrimination question with a "yes" were then asked to give specific examples in which such discrimination takes place. Representative comments from each category of respondees are given below:

Big Businesses

Not placed in training programs on an equal basis with men. Not put into the managerial stream because of reservations about permanence.

Younger women are a greater risk in providing training and planning for future needs of the organization—due to marriage, pregnancy, and relocation of their husbands. But is this discrimination? Males would not be trained for management if their goals were in another field.

Promotional opportunities in management. The climate, however, is improving.

Fewer opportunities for top managerial positions.

On-the-job training, pay and opportunities.

Small Businesses

The line manager is not willing to change. If one can generalize, the older the manager the greater the resistance.

74

Salary and top level positions.

Advancement.

A general feeling that women are less able to direct the work of others from a position of leadership.

Tradition abounds to limit their opportunities to only certain promotions into management positions.

Women in Management

Most women feel this is a man's world. They are not promoted to managerial positions, and they are certainly not hired to such positions initially.

In my own industry (publishing) few women get top jobs—top management conferences pull 100 men to 5 women.

In general, men do not believe that women are serious in their intent to pursue a career, to study, to scheme, to confront, to grow and to "stay with it."

Initial hiring, *salary,* advancement. Only in rare instances are women paid equal salaries for a position usually filled by a male.

Women must convince management of their sincerity and ambition through exemplary performance and determination.

Training for management rarely includes women at submanagerial levels; women are expected to be *extra-ordinary* workers to qualify for management.

I feel that men have always tended to have the higher positions, and that they in general still have the say as to whether or not a woman is promoted. In general, men do not admit that women may have the brains to fill managerial positions. Also, women are not aggressive.

Men zealously guard the management ranks as if they fear an invasion—if they let you in it is always for less salary.

It appears they must start as a secretary rather than going immediately into a management program.

They are blocked mid-point up the ladder of advancement by subconscious and often male prejudice against women in top jobs. They are not even considered for top management spots—seldom are in positions to supervise men.

On-the-job training, pay, job opportunities. Particularly in the South, women are not automatically selected for opinions, committees, or to represent the firm or industry.

Company Formal Policies

Over half of the big business respondees and more than one third of the small business respondees had a formal (stated) policy relative to the employment of women in management (Table XXII). Women in management were also asked this question and, in contrast, almost 95 percent said their company did not have a formal policy. Since the women respondees were not expected to have factual information relative to employment policy and statistics, it can be concluded that women tend to feel their companies do not have formal policies when, in fact, many of them probably do.

Table XXII

EXISTENCE OF FORMAL (STATED) POLICY ON EMPLOYMENT
OF WOMEN IN MANAGEMENT AMONG RESPONDING COMPANIES

Response	Big Businesses		Respondee Classification Small Businesses		Women in Management	
	N	%	N	%	N	%
No Formal Policy	32	39.6	29	46.1	136	94.4
Formal Policy	46	56.7	23	36.5	4	2.8
No Reply	3	3.7	11	17.4	4	2.8

SOURCE: Survey conducted among selected sample of big businesses, small businesses, and women in management.

The respondees who answered the "formal policy" question with a "yes" were then asked to give their stated policy. Representative comments from each category of respondees are given below:

Big Businesses

Simply, we want competent, able people, regardless of race, color, creed, sex, or national origin.

As part of our policy, we do not discriminate on the basis of race, creed, color, or sex.

We hire the most qualified person for any job available, male, female, black, white.

76

Small Businesses

Only stated policy is that of "equal opportunity employer" including nondiscrimination on basis of sex.

This is a business one must know.

There shall be no discrimination against any person or group because of race, religion, age, color, sex, or national origin.

Women in Management

Both men and women must be considered for most positions if they apply.

Off the record, it appears the policy is to promote women because they do not have qualified men. I did not ask for this job, I did not want it and do not need to work, but I knew it was a challenge to prove that women could do it and if I were successful it would mean an opening for a lot of women with our bank. After seven months as manager the record looks extra good as to the progress, growth, and profits.

Our policy is not in written form. It is verbal and at times vociferous. "We welcome women to managerial positions—(we just don't hire them!)."

Female Superiors and Male Subordinates

All three responding categories were asked the question, "Considering all levels of management, how do male subordinates react to female superiors?"

As shown in Table XXIII, no respondee stated "Most men prefer working for a woman." Significantly, over 40 percent of big business respondees checked the answer "No problem, most men don't care whether they work for a man or a woman." Small business respondees, however, were not as liberal, with only 9.5 percent checking "No problem."

Over half of all respondees indicated "Most men prefer working for a man." This was especially true of the small business category, where more than 85 percent of the respondees checked this answer.

Sex Complaints

Big business and small business respondees were asked the question, "Of all complaints relating to discrimination of promotion

77

XXIII

IMPRESSIONS OF RESPONDEES TOWARD REACTION OF MALE SUBORDINATES TO FEMALE SUPERIORS

Respondee Impression	Respondee Classification					
	Big Businesses		Small Businesses		Women in Management	
	N	%	N	%	N	%
"No problem—most men don't care whether they work for a man or a woman."	34	41.9	6	9.5	52	36.2
"Most men prefer working for a woman."	0	0	0	0	0	0
"Most men prefer working for a man."	42	51.9	54	85.8	88	61.1
Companies not responding to question.	5	6.2	3	4.7	4	2.7

SOURCE: Survey conducted among selected sample of big businesses, small businesses, and women in management.

into management since the enactment of Title VII in 1964, what percent were related to: sex? other?" (Table XXIV).

Only slightly more than 2 percent of big business respondees reported having any sex complaints relative to discrimination in pro-

Table XXIV

COMPLAINTS RELATED TO SEX DISCRIMINATION IN PROMOTION INTO MANAGEMENT AMONG RESPONDING COMPANIES SINCE ENACTMENT OF TITLE VII

Type Complaint	Big Businesses		Small Businesses	
	N	%	N	%
Sex	2	2.4	0	0
Other (Race)	35	43.3	23	36.5
Replying None	36	44.4	31	49.2
No Reply	8	9.9	9	14.3

SOURCE: Survey conducted among selected sample of big businesses and small businesses.

motion into management, and no small business respondee reported complaints based on sex. Most complaints filed under Title VII relative to promotion into management have been of a racial nature. (Forty-three percent of the big businesses and 36 percent of the small businesses reported such complaints.) A very substantial share of respondees reported no sex complaints had been filed relative to promotion into management since the enactment of Title VII. It appears that while a very substantial percent of women felt discrimination exists, a very few were sufficiently motivated to file a complaint charging their company with discrimination.

Special Training

All categories of respondees were asked "Does your organization provide any training exclusively for women and for the specific purpose of preparing women to assume management positions or upgrade themselves in management?" (Table XXV).

Both big businesses (83.9 percent) and small businesses (95.2 percent) reported that no special training is provided to train women for management-level positions.

Table XXV

EXISTENCE OF SPECIAL TRAINING TO PREPARE WOMEN TO
ASSUME MANAGEMENT POSITIONS, OR TO UPGRADE THEMSELVES
IN MANAGEMENT AMONG RESPONDING COMPANIES

| Special Training | Respondee Classification | | | |
| | Big Businesses | | Small Businesses | |
	N	%	N	%
Yes	6	7.4	0	0
No	68	83.9	60	95.2
No Answer	7	8.7	3	4.8

SOURCE: Survey conducted among selected sample of big businesses and small businesses.

Effectiveness

Table XXVI reflects the opinions of all three respondee categories toward frequently stated generalizations regarding the effectiveness of women in management. An analysis of respondees to eighteen selected generalizations is given below.

1. *"Women are too emotional in working with other people."*
Over half the big business respondees and almost half of the small

79

Table XXVI

GENERALIZATIONS REGARDING EFFECTIVENESS OF WOMEN IN MANAGEMENT
(Percentages expressed as averages for all respondees within each classification)

Generalizations: Women vs. Men	Respondee Classification								
	TRUE			FALSE			NO REPLY		
	Big Businesses %	Small Businesses %	Women in Management %	Big Businesses %	Small Businesses %	Women in Management %	Big Businesses %	Small Businesses %	Women in Management %
1. Women are too emotional in working with other people.	58.2	46.1	16.4	40.5	51.4	81.4	1.3	2.5	2.2
2. Women have less motivation than men.	78.4	69.3	36.4	19.2	29.2	68.2	2.4	1.5	1.4
3. Women are not as capable in managerial positions as men.	38.0	35.3	21.4	60.9	63.4	77.2	1.1	1.3	1.4
4. Women cannot make precise, clear decisions.	23.1	29.7	11.5	75.1	69.1	86.9	1.8	1.2	1.6
5. Women cannot effectively hire subordinates.	44.6	58.3	20.5	53.3	41.2	77.7	2.1	.5	1.8
6. Women do not have the fortitude to fire subordinate personnel when necessary.	18.1	21.1	5.6	81.2	77.3	93.2	.7	1.6	1.2
7. Women in working with men use femininity to achieve their objectives.	21.6	36.5	10.5	77.2	62.1	87.9	1.2	1.4	1.6

continued

Table XXVI
(continued)

Statement									
8. Women do not provide as much return for investment in educational and training dollars—in other words, their employment patterns are not stable—continuous and with longevity.	89.5	78.6	31.5	9.2	20.1	66.8	1.3	1.3	1.7
9. Women prefer not to work for women. They are competitive with and jealous of other women, so prefer men supervisors.	64.6	54.0	22.6	33.3	44.4	75.5	2.1	1.6	1.9
10. Men prefer not to work for women—they use feminine wiles on one hand and are aggressive and emasculating on the other.	79.4	73.6	37.4	19.4	24.3	59.9	1.2	2.1	2.7
11. Absenteeism among women is higher than men.	31.4	44.7	19.1	67.4	52.9	78.4	1.2	2.4	2.5
12. Women are overly sensitive to contradiction.	23.6	28.7	36.5	75.1	70.1	62.1	1.3	1.2	1.4
13. Women are too personal in giving or receiving criticism.	81.6	76.5	27.5	16.1	21.9	71.1	2.3	1.6	1.4
14. Women do not have a sense of fair play.	16.4	22.4	8.9	80.9	77.2	89.5	2.7	.4	1.6

continued

Table XXVI
(continued)

15. Women work only to supplement income.	21.6	31.5	12.5	76.5	66.6	86.3	2.8	1.9	1.2
16. Women expect special treatment.	17.5	21.6	11.5	80.9	76.9	87.2	1.6	1.5	1.3
17. Women are not as apt to become as totally committed to management as men.	69.5	67.6	41.2	29.3	30.7	57.3	1.2	1.7	1.5
18. Men have careers; women have only jobs—women don't take any deep interest in a career.	71.5	70.4	36.5	27.5	28.4	62.3	1.0	1.2	1.2

business respondees felt women are too emotional in working with other people. But among the women in management who commented on this generalization, only 16.4 percent believed women are too emotional. Obviously, women in management have a different view of female emotionality than do men.

2. *"Women have less motivation than men."* A very substantial majority of big business respondees (78.4 percent) and small business respondees (69.3 percent) agreed that women are not as highly motivated as men. But only slightly more than one third of the women in management respondees felt women have less motivation than men. Again, it is apparent that women have a much different view of their own performance than men.

3. *"Women are not as capable in managerial positions as men."* On this generalization slightly more than one third of big business and small business respondees believed women are not as capable in management, and slightly more than one fifth of the women in management respondees felt women are not as capable as men. Conversely and paradoxically, a large majority of respondees in both big businesses and small businesses categories apparently felt that women are as capable as men in managerial positions.

4. *"Women cannot make precise, clear decisions."* Most respondees in each category agreed that women are decisive. Women in management in particular believed that the generalization "Women cannot make precise, clear decisions," is not true.

5. *"Women cannot effectively hire subordinates."* Women-in-management respondees by almost a four to one majority said women *can* hire subordinates effectively. But about half of the small business respondees and more than two fifths of the big business respondees stated that this generalization is true.

6. *"Women do not have the fortitude to fire subordinate personnel when necessary."* By a large majority each category of respondees agreed that women do have the stamina to dismiss subordinate personnel when necessary. Women in management in particular felt that women can dismiss personnel.

7. *"Women use femininity to achieve objectives."* Most respondees believed this statement is generally false. Only 21.6 percent of the big businesses, 36.5 percent of the small business respondees, and 10.5 percent of women-in-management respondees felt this generalization is true.

8. *"Women do not provide as much return for investment in educational and training dollars—in other words, their employment patterns are not stable—continuous and with longevity."* A majority of the big business respondees (89.5 percent) and 78.6 percent of small business respondees agreed that this statement is true, but women appeared to have a much different view. Only 31.5 percent of the women in management respondees felt the statement is true.

9. *"Women prefer not to work for women. They are competitive with and jealous of other women, so prefer men supervisors."* Here again, big business respondees and small business respondees felt this generalization is true. However, only slightly more than one fifth of the women in management respondees agreed with the statement.

10. *"Men prefer not to work for women—they use feminine wiles on one hand and are aggressive and emasculating on the other."* Again, by substantial majorities, big business respondees and small business respondees felt this generalization is true. Only slightly more than one third of the women-in-management respondees agreed with the statement.

11. *"Absenteeism among women is higher than men."* Less than one third of big business respondees (31.4 percent) and less than one half of small business respondees (44.7 percent) believed this generalization is true. The women-in-management category, which probably did not have access to actual absentee data, by a large majority (78.4 percent) stated that this generalization is false.

12. *"Women are overly sensitive to contradiction."* A higher percent of women in management (36.5 percent) felt this generalization is true than was the case of either the big business category (23.6 percent) or the small business respondee category (28.7 percent).

13. *"Women are too personal in giving or receiving criticism."* Big business respondees (81.6 percent) and small business respondees (76.5 percent) agreed with the generalization that "women are too personal in giving or receiving criticism." Most women in management respondees (71.1 percent), however, thought the generalization is false.

14. *"Women do not have a sense of fair play."* The majority of all respondees in each category agreed that this generalization is

not true. But women in management by a much larger percent of respondees felt women do have a sense of fair play.

15. *"Women work only to supplement income."* Women in management by eight to one said "no." Almost seven out of ten small business respondees said "no," and almost four out of five big business respondees said "no." Apparently, it is widely felt among business executives that additional income is not the only factor explaining why women work at the management level.

16. *"Women expect special treatment."* Among all categories of respondees, there was an overwhelming "no" to this.

17. *"Women are not as totally committed to management as men."* More than two thirds of big business respondees (69.5 percent) and small business respondees (67.6 percent) agreed with this generalization. More than two fifths of women in management respondees (41.2 percent) also felt that "women are not as apt to become as totally committed to management as men."

18. *"Men have careers; women have only jobs—women don't take any deep interest in a career, so they don't think in large terms about the scope of their careers."* This generalization, which was similar to the commitment to management generalization, was considered true by more than seven out of ten of both big business (71.5 percent) and small business (70.4 percent) respondees. Slightly more than one third (36.5 percent) of the women-in-management respondees also agreed that "women don't take any deep interest in a career so they don't think in large terms about the scope of their careers."

Recommendations

The final question asked of all respondees was: "If you believe discrimination exists toward women in management, what do you recommend, in general, should be done to eliminate this discrimination (a) by individual companies or organizations, and (b) by women interested in a career in management?"

Big business respondees tended to be more cooperative in answering this open-end question (41.4 percent) than small business (26.3 percent). However, not only did most women in management (87.5 percent) respond to the question, they contributed more lengthy and detailed recommendations.

Recommendations made by the three respondee categories were closely related. A summary of the recommendations made, together with selected verbatim comments, is provided below:

Recommendation 1. Management should make a more conscious effort to seek out qualified women. Many of the small business and big business respondees indicated that if a woman is well qualified and performs in a professional manner, most companies are glad to have her in management. The key, however, is professional and academic training and competency. Typical comments made primarily by women in management were:

> Stop looking at women as a separate sex and judge each applicant individually on his or her qualifications and merit. Open top management jobs to women and not rule them out at middle management levels.

> Top management jobs should be opened to women and women should be considered on the same basis as men — talent, knowledge of the problem, company loyalty — whatever.

> Set up specific standards on all levels which men and women are expected to abide by — and make these published guidelines.

> An open-minded attitude toward women in management with opportunity available on ability. Hire them and give them a chance in assistant capacity to prove ability for management responsibility.

Recommendation 2. Women who desire a career in management should be willing to make a lifetime commitment. Predominant among the responding executives was the attitude that the way conditions are, a company is more than happy to have a good worker, conscientious and reliable, without discriminating against women. She will be accepted if she can prove her worth to the company by doing the job and demonstrating dedication. Women must, however, be willing to accept responsibility, to put the job first, even over family when necessary. As one executive stated, "The job has to become a way of life and not just a forty-hour-a-week job. This means full interest and dedication with a definite attitude of continuous and stable employment."

Recommendation 3. Ignore sex and adopt a promotional policy based strictly on ability. A general theme of all respondees, but in particular the women in management, was "judge people on their merits, regardless of sex." However, it was the feeling of women in management and many of the small business and big business respondees that "women have to be much smarter and must work twice as hard as a man in the same work to gain equal opportunities."

Comments illustrating the feelings among the respondees are as follows:

No person whether male or female should be deprived of their civil rights and should reject any regulation that would do so.

Women should be on an equal pay scale with men in relation to their education, training, and initiative. I have seen many women who actually have had more education, more training, and as much initiative as some men but who do not receive the same amount of pay as men in the same position. I feel that is the most unfair practice and cannot see why women in the past have stood for it. They should not accept a second-class status in business.

Our problems will not be fully resolved until the concept of humanpower transcends manpower or womanpower, and the value of each individual's potential for productivity becomes the paramount concern. While laws have confirmed that sex is in the worker, not the work, social attitudes continue to uphold the "feminine mystique" of woman as wife, mother, and homemaker. A re-ordering of social structure will be necessary—and will, I believe, inevitably occur—based on the premise that men, as well as women, are mates, parents, and cultural time-finders (and have responsibilities in these areas). There will need to be broad recognition of the basic truth that, while woman's body is her own, reproduction is a bi-sexual function; that home-children-family-life has requirements and rewards for both sexes. Meanwhile, companies, organizations, and individuals must work to creat opportunities for women in management (and heretofore exclusive or elitely male functions) in the same fashion as they are being created for the black citizen and other minority groups—by education, encouragement, coercion, and insistence, where necessary. The first step is to find enough people who care!

Recommendation 4. Provide special management training for women. In support of this recommendation, the following representative comments were made:

87

Men are hired with the idea that they will progress to managers. Women aren't. Women are hired to be permanent clerks. Women have to work twice as hard to go half as far as men.

Definitely provide management training programs for women.

Females should be treated in such a manner as to incite a deep feeling of interest, equality, initiative and need. This includes making on-the-job training and other training available to women as well as men.

Recommendation 5. Educate top management about how to utilize women effectively in management jobs. Many respondees who answered this question felt it would take some time for men to become reconciled to the fact that some women desire careers in business strongly enough to educate themselves and in other ways prepare themselves to fill responsible positions. Some respondees went so far as to suggest promoting the effective use of women in management-level jobs within the company and outside the company through public relations programs. Comments to this effect, for example, were:

> Set a good example and PR it to the hilt! Get pilot companies to honor and exploit successful women and get publicity where men can see it.

> Create openings not previously available to women. Need women to represent their industry to other groups.

> Those companies who have successful women VIPs should be encouraged to brag about it to the press and TV. Perhaps someone should write a best seller.

Recommendation 6. Create a professional awareness in women relative to a career in management. Neither small business, large business, nor women in management respondees overlooked the necessity for basic professional preparation. Almost all of the respondees shared essentially the feelings expressed in the following representative comments:

> More education and more interest in workings of the organization—more dedication.

> Show interest. Ask to be sent to schools which will assist women in their careers. Their male counterparts do not hesitate to ask.

Women must be willing to study, to persist, to take every opportunity to advance, and, when the opportunity comes, to prove that they are capable, both for themselves and for other women.

They should seek advancement by adequate, even over-adequate, qualifications in the areas of education, training, experience, and on-the-job abilities.

Acquire knowledge and skill. Learn to be inwardly free as a person. Continually seek a high degree of interpersonal competence. Real charm—and I strongly advocate it for men and women—is based on sincerity.

Control emotions, work hard, show interest in job, study, assume responsibility.

Recommendation 7. Encourage women to seek out those companies that do not discriminate at the management level. Several respondees felt women should take advantage of companies which are liberal in their employment and promotion policies related to utilization of women at management levels. These recommendations can be summed up by this descriptive comment:

Apply for jobs in companies with liberal employment policies toward women—and then do a damn good job. The reluctant managements, then, can draw from the example set and eventually relax their employment practices toward women.

Recommendation 8. Encourage women to throw away feelings of male dominance. Some respondees suggested that women sometimes stifle their opportunities by failing to disregard the attitudes that women cannot perform as effectively as men at the management levels.

Women were urged to:

Rid themselves of the feeling that pertains to a position labeled "for men only" and to make a stand to break barriers relating to positions of this kind.

Women have made great progress in the field of business but not enough. They need to literally "throw away" feelings of male dominance in business. Quite a few women still have these feelings. The idea that most managerial positions are "for men only" still exists to some extent among most women in our country. Women must obtain more initiative and maintain interest in their jobs and in the business world.

Push for an equal opportunity credo for private industry that applies not just to Negroes but *also* to women.

Push for it—become super valuable—then move on it—but never with an aggressive act. Work hard—work creatively—be fun—don't gossip with other female employees and league with them. Be an individual!

Recommendation 9. Simply let Title VII take its course. Several big business and small business respondees felt that the new law (Title VII) will improve opportunities for women in management, but improvement will require time. Some respondees indicated the specific efforts their companies are making to contribute to the improvement of utilization of women in management. However, the following qualification was generally shared by respondees:

It is unquestionably true that greater utilization will be made of female talent as time goes on. While the enactment of Title VII in 1964 had some effect on the growth since then, I think any major improvement is more directly related to the progressive movement in our society and businesses' need for even more talent.

Another respondee had this to say:

To do something about the discrimination means treating a symptom. Our socio-economic system is, whether we like it or don't, neurotic. Discrimination of any kind is a defense mechanism. If our society were healthy, more in congruence with the organic base for an organized valuing process, it would not feel compelled to make use of devices, pretenses, techniques, etc., as it does. Organizations will have to develop changed attitudes. An "extending" program is needed. Extending of minds; self-enhancing to individuals and, as a result self-enhancing to the organizations they serve. A more "natural" valuing process is absolutely necessary for the survival and evolution of the human species. The credibility gaps which our system, including its firms and organizations, has produced are being challenged with revolution today. A basic realignment must occur; and women of management caliber may well become the yeast in the dough. For they have become more keenly aware of their imposed limitations.

Women can bring about stronger reforms concerning the Civil Rights Act of 1964 if they would only use their legal rights to the fullest extent.

Title VII, time, and nature will take its course!

Chapter VII

CONCLUSIONS AND RECOMMENDATIONS

This study of business executives' attitudes toward women in top management positions in business organizations has resulted in the following conclusions:

(1) *There may be reason to question the sometime-quoted statement that women constitute no more than 2 percent of management personnel in the United States.* While the survey samples used in this study are not necessarily typical of the total universe, it was found that well over half of all respondees reported more than 2 percent of their management personnel were women. Perhaps the figure, 2 percent, refers to senior executives only.

(2) *The majority of women now employed in management work at the first or supervisory level.* A significant proportion of small businesses (18.7 percent) and big businesses (29.6 percent) indicated the majority of women now employed in managerial positions are at the middle level, and only 1.2 percent of the big businesses reported women at senior management levels. In small businesses no female senior executive personnel were reported.

(3) *Utilization of women in line management has changed little since enactment of Title VII.* Over 60 percent of all respondees reported no change in utilization of women since 1964. However, many more companies reported an increase in utilization of women in management than reported a decrease in utilization since 1964.

(4) *Changes in the utilization of women in staff management capacities since 1964 has followed the same general pattern as utilization of women in line capacities.* Again, well over 60 percent of all respondees reported no change since 1964. However, increases in utilization of women in staff capacities considerably exceeded decreases.

(5) *Women in management tend to view the emotional side of women much differently than men.* Specifically, women as revealed in this study view themselves as being more intuitive, more intelligent, more logical, and more dedicated than men view them.

(6) *Data developed in this study indicate women have made the greatest penetration into management in big businesses in general administration, data processing, accounting, and production.*

Meanwhile, in small businesses women have made their greatest penetration in production, followed by administration, accounting and sales.

(7) *A large majority of both big businesses and small businesses reported their experience in utilization of women in management as either being "very good" or "good."* Few respondees stated their experience as "excellent" or "poor."

(8) *Less than 8 percent of big business and small business respondees reported "more women are seeking management jobs."* Since the enactment of Title VII, the majority of respondees indicated "no noticeable difference."

(9) *Almost half of the big business respondees and 76 percent of the small business respondees said discrimination against women in management does in fact exist.* Specific areas mentioned in which this discrimination takes place include on-the-job training, pay, promotion, and initial consideration for acceptance into management. Most of the discrimination was reported as "subtle" rather than obvious.

(10) *Over half of the big business respondees and more than one third of the small business respondees claim to have a formal or stated policy relative to the employment of women in management.* This policy usually is simply a statement that "we want competent, able people regardless of race, creed, color, sex, or national origin."

(11) *Data developed from this study indicate that "most men prefer working for a man."* Meanwhile, a substantial share of big business respondees (41.9 percent) said "no problem, most men don't care whether they work for a man or a woman."

(12) *Only slightly more than 2 percent of big business respondees reported having any complaints relative to sex discrimination in promotion into management, and no small business respondees reported such a complaint.* It appears that, while a very substantial percent of women feel discrimination exists (70 percent), very few have been sufficiently motivated to file a complaint with the company charging discrimination.

(13) *Overwhelming majorities of big businesses (83.9 percent) and small businesses (95.2 percent) reported no special training is provided women for management-level positions.*

(14) *Data developed from this study revealed that both big business and small business respondees tend to react in much the*

same manner to the common generalizations frequently made relative to the performance of women in management. Women-in-management respondees tend to perceive themselves as different from the way they are perceived by big business and small business respondees.

It can be concluded that either a majority or a very significant percent of big business and small business respondees feel:

(a) Women are too emotional in working with other women.
(b) Women have less motivation than men.
(c) Women cannot effectively hire subordinates.
(d) Women do not provide as large a return on investment in educational and training dollars as men.
(e) Women prefer *not* to work for other women.
(f) Men prefer *not* to work for women.
(g) Women are *not* as dedicated to management as men.
(h) Women are *not* career oriented.

At the same time, more than one half of both big business and small business respondees felt that:

(a) Women are as capable in management positions as men.
(b) Women can make precise, clear decisions.
(c) Women do have the fortitude to dismiss subordinate personnel.
(d) Women do *not* use femininity to achieve objectives.
(e) Absenteeism among women is *not* higher than for men.
(f) Women are *not* overly sensitive to contradiction.
(g) Women do have a sense of fair play.
(h) Women do *not* work only to supplement income.
(i) Women do *not* expect special treatment.

Based on both secondary data, as presented in preceding chapters, and survey research, the following recommendations relative to this study are submitted:

(1) Additional research appears needed to pinpoint the specific reasons behind the apparent apathy of women in management with regard to making formal and informal complaints under Title VII of the Civil Rights Act relative to the advancement of women into management. It appears unrealistic to assume that the insignificant number of complaints lodged thus far under Title VII indicates the true situation with regard to equality of treatment of both sexes at the management level of business. If such research develops the fact that fear is the principal factor which

limits filing of complaints, then additional federal legislation may be needed to guarantee no reprisals for those who make complaints.

(2) It would appear that training designed specifically to prepare women for management positions might well be worth consideration by both businesses and universities. Nowhere in the literature and in none of the comments volunteered by respondees was there found to be any concerted effort to develop managerial abilities in women. Such training, if it proves successful, might help significantly in better utilization of women in management.

(3) Wider publication by business of job opportunities at the management level for women seems in order. The concept of "equal opportunity employer" appears to be essentially limited in meaning to race, although in fact it does include sex. Concurrently, a more aggressive recruitment policy on the part of business to urge women to make application for management level positions seems wise.

(4) From the original data collected in this study, it is apparent that certain generalizations which indicate less adequate performance on the part of women in management when compared with men are held as true by many respondees. It is believed important that research be conducted to ascertain more precisely whether in fact women are different from men in management potential, ability, and performance.

(5) Women who desire careers in management are advised to seek employment in those organizations which are most liberal in the recruitment and promotion of women into management. The study revealed that company practices vary widely in utilization of women in management, even for companies within the same industrial classification.

(6) Based on the assumption that the goal of our economic society is to utilize to the fullest possible extent individual resources and capabilities, it appears to be in the interests of national economic policy for business organizations to study carefully recruitment policies relative to management personnel to determine whether the goals of the individual businesses could better be achieved in terms of economy and effectiveness through wider utilization of women in management. As former President Johnson stated, "The greatest waste of talent is womanpower." Many businesses could possibly achieve more effectiveness by more extensive utilization of women in management.

Epilogue

A BREAKTHROUGH BY 1980?

The black revolutionaires, student activists, poverty protestors, anti-war demonstrators, and now rumors of rebellious women make up today's scene. And the rebellion of women could be the most important of all. The blacks make up only 10 percent of our population, students 15 percent, the poor 5 percent, the anti-war revolutionaries 7 percent; but women are over half our population. If women revolt, all of us will take notice; for, how women vote can determine who is president, how women spend money can determine the direction of our economy. Already women have more potential behind-the-scenes power than perhaps they know.

The thought of masses of angry women is frightening. It goes against all culturally induced ideals of feminine decorum; but more than that, it involves a population majority who already, from recent dissenters, know the power of protest. Will they use it? Or, perhaps a better question, why are women so uneasy?

More sophisticated, well-educated, and experienced (vicariously if not actually) women are less and less satisfied with being just sexy, sexier females. Increasingly, they feel a deeper and more basic personal need for growth and achievement as persons. Most women now work from necessity, but many who seek fulfillment at the top levels do not have to work. In a sense, they could stay in their ivied, suburban castles, splendidly isolated from world problems; rather, more and more of those women choose to get bloodied in the economic skirmishes of living.

Within ten years women will account for a substantial number of all management employees. Our society and business world, hopefully, is reaching a new maturity. But, more than this, brainpower has replaced muscle power as a national resource. And, as never before, these are changing times. Since World War II, there has been more technological and intellectual change than in the previous history of the world. In 1945 more progress began to be made in a week than had been made in a year. For centuries the assumption could be made that each generation would die in essentially the same environment as it had been born. The physical environment might change a little, but the social and moral environment would be about the same. This is no longer true. Each succeeding year brings still more technological progress.

Never has there been a greater need to use all brain resources than now and in the coming years. The National Manpower Council in a study of our nation's total manpower resources emphasizes that only one one-hundredth of a percent (that's only one in a thousand) of the human race makes new discoveries. Only a slightly larger percent significantly contributes to progress. A quick survey shows a surplus of routine workers; there is a hundred times as much competition for "little" jobs as for big ones. And everyday technology destroys more of these repetitive jobs and creates new ones at higher and higher levels. Increasingly, competent people are needed at middle and top occupational levels without regard to sex, if a better world is to be a reality. Discrimination against women in job assignments, training and promotion, affects employers and our total economy as much as it does women. To fail to maintain the pace is to come out second-rate as a nation.

The next ten years, however, will not necessarily be one of easy transition. Growing demands for equal participation run headlong into deeply rooted age-old myths of women's place and stereotypes of women's potential. This period will be in the midst of changing cultural and social values, a confusing time for many who find themselves torn between tradition and new ways. Society suffers from a tendency to fight change, especially when it involves basic ways of thinking and living. And women on the verge of a new life affect basic male-female relationships (man as a husband, as a father, as a male; woman as a wife, as a mother, as a female) and make both men and women nervous. However, we need to recognize that society is on the verge of a new life and then work together for a healthier society. Our recent social crises revolve around the quality of human life and the chance for each individual to develop his full potential. Sexism is only a small part of a bigger revolution of values turning head over heels.

But all this does not mean to imply that *all* women want to work outside the home, or that all women are willing to make long-range career commitments which top level occupations require, or that they should. The life objective of many women is still, and will be yet for some time, marriage and family only. There are other women, however, who do want a career and do have the drive, industry, willingness to accept responsibility, dedication,

97

loyalty, and all other characteristics necessary to a demanding careers. (Despite the book, **How to Succeed in Business Without Really Trying,** there is no other way.) Many men do not want top executive positions either. Others do not have the necessary characteristics to qualify for top executive positions. These ambitionless men do not affect other men who are committed to going as far as they can go. Women want this same opportunity, too; not equality with men (a thorny notion). Men and women cannot be "equal"—they are basically and biologically different. But they do need and want recognition of their value and uniqueness. The goal is not to make women more like men, or men more like women, but for everyone to become most like themselves. Nor is the goal male-female competition. Rather, the challenge is for the male and female to complement each other and add his and her part to the whole, increasing the richness of human resources. All people have many unrealized potentialities which will greatly enhance the world, and themselves, if they develop them.

Some of the best breaks for women appear to be in companies where young men predominate, or in a young company, or in a young industry. Many young men, perhaps undaunted by fears of unisex, seem to prefer a cooperative life style. One such young businessman, an enlightened southeastern executive, said, "The basic differences toward women in business are probably more a result of attitudes that have been built up over a period of time. I have an idea that if women were accepted without regard to sex and allowed to progress without regard to sex, they would probably fall into the same emotional, intellectual, and dependability patterns of men."

He went on to say, "The men who do complain about women in top positions have never worked with women who hold responsible positions. Once they do, they lose their biases. There are no measurable and important differences between men and women with respect to intelligence, ability, and aptitude. Attitudes at home, at work, and by society have been the roadblocks."

In the future, then, men and women may enter a shared sphere— a small step in human evolution. But, in the words of Lao-Tsze, "The journey of a thousand miles begins with one step."

Appendix A

RESEARCH METHOD

Primary data were collected to determine the degree to which discrimination exists toward women at the management level in business. An effort was made to answer the following broad questions:

(1) What is the degree of discrimination toward women in management?

(2) Has Title VII decreased discrimination on the basis of sex?

(3) What are the attitudes and existing business practices of business leaders toward utilization of women in management?

(4) Is the nature of discrimination against women principally "legal" or is it mainly "subtle?"

(5) What problems stand in the way of fuller utilization of women in management?

Selection of large businesses. The Fortune Directory (June 15, 1968) comprised the universe population for the large businesses. The **Directory** consists of the 500 largest United States industrial corporations, the 50 largest banks, 50 largest merchandising firms, 50 transportation companies, 50 largest life-insurance companies, and 50 largest utility companies.

A total of 300 firms were selected from these 750 American companies, 50 each from industrial corporations, banks, merchandising firms, transportation companies, life-insurance companies, utility companies. The 50 industrial corporations were selected randomly from the 500 industrial corporations by using a Table of Random Digits. The mail questionnaire was directed to either the president or vice president for personnel at the companies' main offices.

Selection of small businesses. Three hundred small businesses (small as defined by the Small Business Administration)[1] were surveyed. These companies paralleled, as nearly as possible, the large businesses: 50 each were selected from industrial corporations, small merchandising firms, small transportation companies, small life-insurance companies, and small utility companies. The firms were selected randomly from trade directories, using a Table of Random Digits.

The mail questionnaire was directed to either the president, owner, manager, or vice-president-personnel, or personnel director, as appropriate, for the particular company.

Selection of women in management. This study might have been incomplete, or at least one-sided, without the opinions of women in management. Therefore, 300 women employed in management positions were surveyed. Size of company was not a factor in defining this population sample, and both large and small businesses were represented. The sample was selected from trade directories and **Who's Who in American Women.**

Construction of the questionnaire. Identical questionnaires were used for the large and small businesses. The questionnaire sent to women was modified slightly to gain a woman's point of view.

Respondees in both big businesses and small businesses were individuals assumed to have access to detailed employment data. Women-in-management respondees were not necessarily personnel executives but rather were selected only because they were known to hold management positions. Consequently, accuracy of factual information supplied by women executives in some cases must be considered an estimate. Certain questions were not asked women in management because it was assumed they would not have first-hand information at their disposal to answer the question with validity.

The questionnaire contained nineteen questions. The majority of the questions were objective, requiring either a "yes" or "no" answer or "check." Many questions, however, provided the respondee an opportunity to comment or qualify his answer if he felt it necessary.

These qualifications and comments, as well as the write-in answers to open-end questions, were significant in adding a qualitative dimension to the findings.

Questionnaire returns. The number of companies responding to the questionnaire for big businesses totaled 81, or a 27 percent return. Small businesses' response was slightly lower, totaling 63 returns, or a 23 percent return. The greatest return, however, came from the women-in-management population, with 144 responses, or a 48 percent return.

Appendix B

QUESTIONNAIRES

To Business Firms

SPECIAL SURVEY

AN EVALUATION OF THE APPLICATION AND
IMPLEMENTATION OF TITLE VII AS IT APPLIES TO
WOMEN IN MANAGEMENT

Please Return To:

GEORGIA STATE COLLEGE
P. O. Box 100
33 Gilmer Street, S.E.
Atlanta, Georgia 30303

YOUR NAME_____

POSITION_____

COMPANY_____

ADDRESS_____

(Please note your comments are totally confidential.)

1. Approximately what percent of your management personnel at all levels is female? _____%

2. Approximately what percent of your management personnel for the management levels indicated below is female?
   Senior level (V. P. or above) _____%
   Middle management _____%
   First level (supervisory) _____%

3. Of all women classified as management, approximately what percent are line? _____% Staff? _____%

4. How has the percent of line management positions filled by women changed since the enactment of Title VII in 1964?
Down by approximately _____%
No perceptible change _____
Up by approximately _____%

5. How has the percent of staff management positions filled by women changed since the enactment of Title VII in 1964?
Down by approximately _____%
No perceptible change _____
Up by approximately _____%

6. What percent of management personnel (line and staff) in each of the functional areas below is female? (Approximate)

Accounting	_____%	Data Processing	_____%
Finance	_____%	Administrative	_____%
Sales	_____%	Other_____	_____%
Production	_____%		

7. Based on your experience, when compared with men are women in management more:

	Yes	No	No Difference
Intuitive?	_____	_____	_____
Emotional?	_____	_____	_____
Intelligent?	_____	_____	_____
Ambitious?	_____	_____	_____
Logical?	_____	_____	_____
Dedicated?	_____	_____	_____

8. How many formal (submitted in writing) sex discrimination complaints have been lodged against your company since the enactment of Title VII in 1964?

_____

9. Have any of these complaints been carried to a federal agency? Yes_____ No_____
If yes, how many?_____ Disposition_____

_____

(If needed, please attach extra pages of explanation.)

10. As a generalization, which phrase below best describes your company's experience with women in management?

    _____ "Excellent. Women in general perform very well in management—often better than men."

    _____ "Very good. Women do a fine job—equal to men."

    _____ "Good. No real problems or complaints."

    _____ "Poor. Women just don't adjust to responsibilities of management."

11. Since the enactment of Title VII in 1964, how has the interest of women changed in seeking management positions?

    _____ Many more women are seeking management jobs.

    _____ More, but not substantially so.

    _____ No noticeable difference.

    _____ Actually, women seem to be less interested in seeking management jobs than before.

12. Not considering only your own company but American business in general, do you feel women are discriminated against in management?

    Yes_____   No_____

If yes, in what specific ways?_____

_____

_____

(If needed, please attach extra pages of explanation)

13. Does your company have a stated policy on employment of women in management?

    Yes_____   No_____

If yes, what is this stated policy?_____

_____

_____

14. Considering all levels of management, how do male subordinates react to female superiors?

    _____ "No problem. Most men don't care whether they work for a man or a woman."

    _____ "Most men would prefer to work for a woman."

    _____ "Most men would rather work for a man."

15. At which levels of management do men most readily work for a female superior?

_____ Senior level (V. P. or above)

_____ Middle management

_____ First level (supervisory)

16. Of all complaints relating to discrimination of promotion into management since the enactment of Title VII in 1964, what percent were related to:

Sex?____%   Other_____ ____%

17. Does your organization provide any forms of training exclusively for women and for the specific purpose of preparing women to assume management positions or to upgrade themselves in management?

Yes_____   No_____

If yes please describe briefly:_____

_____

_____

18. Below are several generalizations regarding the effectiveness of women in management. For each item, check which you feel most closely approximates your experiences:

Generalizations	Generally True	Generally False
1. Women are too emotional in working with other people.		
2. Women have less motivation than men.		
3. Women are not as capable in managerial positions as men.		

4. Women cannot make precise, clear decisions.

5. Women cannot effectively hire subordinates.

6. Women do not have the fortitude to fire subordinate personnel when necessary.

7. Women in working with men use femininity to achieve their objectives.

8. Women do not provide as much return for investment in educational and training dollars—in other words, their employment patterns are not stable—continuous and with longevity.

9. Women prefer not to work for women. They are competitive with and are jealous of other women, so prefer men supervisors.

10. Men prefer not to work for women—they use feminine wiles on one hand and are aggressive and emasculating on the other.

11. Absenteeism among women is higher than men.

12. Women are overly sensitive to contradiction.

13. Women are too personal in giving or receiving criticism.

14. Women work only to supplement income.

16. Women expect special treatment.

17. Women are not as apt to become as totally committed to management as men.

Generalizations	Generally True	Generally False

18. Men have careers; women
    have only jobs—women
    don't take any deep
    interest in a career, so
    they don't think in large
    terms about the scope
    of their careers.

19. If you believe discrimination exists toward women in man-
    agement, what do you recommend, in general, should be
    done to eliminate this discrimination?
    By individual companies or organizations:_____

    _____

    _____

    _____

    _____

    By women interested in a career in management:_____

    _____

    _____

    _____

    _____

To Women in Management

SPECIAL SURVEY

AN EVALUATION OF THE APPLICATION AND
IMPLEMENTATION OF TITLE VII AS IT APPLIES TO
WOMEN IN MANAGEMENT

Please Return To:

GEORGIA STATE COLLEGE
P. O. Box 100
33 Gilmer Street, S.E.
Atlanta, Georgia 30303

YOUR NAME_____

POSITION_____

COMPANY_____

ADDRESS_____

(Please Note Your Comments Are Totally Confidential)

1. What percent of the total employment in your organization
   is female?   _____%

2. What percent of total *management* personnel do you estimate is female?   _____%

3. How long have you been employed in management?_____
   Your age?_____
   Are you a college graduate? Yes_____   No_____
   Is your position line_____ or staff?_____

4. In general, would you say women desiring to enter man-
   agement in your organization have:
   Good opportunity   _____
   Limited opportunity   _____
   Excellent opportunity   _____

5. How has the percent of management positions filled by women in your company changed since enactment of Title VII in 1964?

   No perceptible change   ———————

   Up by approximately   ———————%

   Down by approximately   ———————%

6. Do women in management positions in your organization tend to supervise primarily other women?———————— men and women about equally?———————— Primarily men only?————————

7. Do you feel there is a shortage of qualified women for managerial positions in your organization?

   Yes———————— No————————

   If yes, explain:————————————————————————————

   ——

   ——

8. Do you feel discrimination exists toward hiring and promotion of women at the management level in your company?

   Yes———————— No————————

   If yes, to what degree? ————————Considerable ————————Minor

                                   ————————Very Considerable

9. Based on your knowledge, how many formal (submitted in writing) sex discrimination complaints have been filed by women against your company since the enactment of Title VII in 1964?————————————————————————————

10. Have you ever filed a formal complaint (one submitted in writing)? Yes———————— No————————

11. Presently, what is the highest position in management occupied by a woman in your organization?————————————————

12. Assuming equal professional competency, in all honesty, would you prefer to work for a man———— or a woman?————

13. Do you feel, generally, that women are as capable at holding a managerial position as men? Yes———————— No————————

14. Based on your experience, when compared with men are women in management more:

	Yes	No	No Difference
Intuitive?	_____	_____	_____
Emotional?	_____	_____	_____
Intelligent?	_____	_____	_____
Ambitious?	_____	_____	_____
Logical?	_____	_____	_____
Dedicated?	_____	_____	_____

15. Not considering only your own company but American business in general, do you feel women are discriminated against in management?   Yes_____   No_____

    If yes, in what specific ways?_____

    _____

    _____

16. Does your company have a stated policy on employment of women in management?   Yes_____   No_____

    If yes, what is this stated policy?_____

    _____

    _____

    (Please use extra pages, if necessary, to define your company policy.)

17. Based on your observations and considering all levels of management, how do male subordinates react to female superiors?

    _____ "No problem. Most men don't care whether they work for a man or a woman."

    _____ "Most men prefer to work for a man."

    _____ "Most men prefer to work for a woman."

110

18. At which levels of management do men most readily work for a female supervisor?

_____ Senior Level (V.P. or above)

_____ Middle management

_____ First level (supervisory)

Generalizations	Generally True	Generally False
1. Women are too emotional in working with other people.		
2. Women have less motivation than men.		
3. Women are not as capable in managerial positions as men.		
4. Women cannot make precise, clear decisions.		
5. Women cannot effectively hire subordinates.		
6. Women do not have the fortitude to fire subordinate personnel when necessary.		
7. Women in working with men use femininity to achieve their objectives.		

8. Women do not provide as much return for investment in educational and training dollars—in other words their employment patterns are not stable—continuous and with longevity.

9. Women prefer not to work for women. They are competitive with and jealous of other women, so prefer men supervisors.

10. Men prefer not to work for women—they use feminine wiles on one hand and are aggressive and emasculating on the other.

11. Absenteeism among women is higher than men.

12. Women are overly sensitive to contradiction.

13. Women are too personal in giving or receiving criticism.

14. Women do not have a sense of fair play.

15. Women work only to supplement income.

Generalizations	Generally True	Generally False

16. Women expect special treatment.

17. Women are not as apt to become as totally committed to management as men.

18. Men have careers; women have jobs. Women don't take any deep interest in a career; they don't think in large terms about the scope of their careers.

19. If you believe discrimination exists toward women in management, what do you recommend, in general, should be done to eliminate this discrimination?

By individual companies or organizations:_____

_____

_____

_____

By women interested in a career in management:_____

_____

_____

_____

FOOTNOTES

Chapter I:

[1] Ruth Brine (Contributing Editor), "The New Feminists: Revolt Against Sexism," *Time,* November 21, 1969.

Chapter II:

[1] Mary R. Beard, *Women as Force in History: A Study in Traditions and Realities* (New York: The Macmillan Company, 1946), p. 275.

[2] George Francois Renard, *Guilds in the Middle Ages to 1919* (New York: A. A. Knopf, 1926).

[3] Beard, *op. cit.,* p. 255.

[4] *Ibid.,* p. 78.

Chapter III:

[1] National Manpower Council, *Womanpower* (New York: Columbia University Press, 1957).

[2] U. S. Department of Labor, *1965 Handbook on Women Workers* (Washington: U. S. Government Printing Office).

[3] Marilyn Mercer, "Is There Room at the Top?" *The Saturday Evening Post,* June 31, 1968.

[4] "EEOC Analysis Shows Few Women in Top Jobs," News release for American newspapers, Thursday, October 19, 1967.

[5] New York City was chosen because it is a "white-collar" city and its 2.4 million white-collar workers accounted for 59 percent of the total employment in 1965.

[6] Equal Employment Opportunity Commission, *Employment Opportunities for Minorities in New York City: An Introduction,* January, 1968.

[7] *Ibid.*

[8] Elizabeth Shelton, "Few Women Hold Key Jobs," *Washington, D. C. Post,* September 2, 1968.

[9] G. W. Bowman, N. B. Worthy, and S. A. Greyser, "Are Women Executives People?" *Harvard Business Review,* July-August 1965.

[10] In an address to the 40th annual Georgia Press Institute in Athens, Georgia, February 1968.

[11] The University of Chicago, Graduate School of Business, the Health Information Foundation, "The Economic Costs of Absenteeism," *Progress in Health Service* (Chicago: University of Chicago Press, March-April, 1963).

[12] Bowman, Worthy, Greyser, *op. cit.*

Chapter IV:

[1] "Southern Senators Fight to Divide Forces Backing Rights Bill," *Wall Street Journal,* March 24, 1964, p. 13.

[2] 88th Congress, 2nd Session, *Congressional Record* (Washington: Government Printing Office, 1964), Vol. 110, Part 2, p. 2577.

[3] *Ibid.*

[4] *Ibid.*

[5] *Ibid.*

[6] "Southern Senators," *op. cit.,* p. 13.

[7] Equal Employment Opportunity Commission, "Facts about Title VII of the Civil Rights Act of 1964" (Washington, D. C.: U. S. Government Printing Office, 1968).

[8] *The Civil Rights Act of 1964, Title VII,* Section 7003, Paragraph 112, 78 Stat. 241, Public Law 88-352.

[9] *The Civil Rights Act of 1964,* Public Law 88-352, 88th Congress, July 2, 1964, p. 1.

[10] Equal Opportunity Commission, U. S. Department Of Labor, *Guidelines on Sex Discrimination Provisions of Title VII of the Civil Rights Act.*

[11] Elizabeth Shelton, "Civil Rights Act Opens More Jobs for Women," *The Atlanta Journal,* November 27, 1966.

Chapter V:

[1] Sonia Pressman, Senior Attorney, EEOC, in an address, "A Man and a Woman—Who Gets the Job?" January 23, 1969.

[2] Equal Employment Opportunity Commission, Washington, D. C.

[3] Equal Employment Opportunity Commission, *Third Annual Report,* 1968 (Washington: U. S. Government Printing Office).

[4] Statement made by Western Electric at hearings before the United States Equal Employment Opportunity Commission on Discrimination in White-Collar Employment, New York, January 15-18, 1968.

[5] *Bowe* v. *Colgate-Palmolive Company,* 56 LC para. 9069 (S. D., Ind., New Albany Division, June 30, 1967).

[6] Pressman, *op. cit.*

[7] *Federal Register,* Volume 33, No. 158, Title 29, Section 1604.4 (August 14, 1968).

[8] Equal Employment Opportunity Commission news release, February 3, 1969, "EEOC Guideline on Classified Advertising Now in Effect."

[9] *Commissioners' Decisions,* 401:501 (7-31-66) and *General Counsel's Opinions,* 401:3033 (5-11-67) (Washington: Bureau of National Affairs, 1966).

[10] Sylvia Porter, "Maternity Leave Policies Illegal, Employer to Find," *Atlanta Journal,* February 28, 1967.

[11] Equal Employment Opportunity Commission, Case No. AT 6-9-603 (6-8-6975).

[12] Sonia Pressman, letter dated October 3, 1968, to author.

[13] *Ibid.,* letter dated February 28, 1969.

[14] Mercer, *op. cit.*

Chapter VI:

1 For a detailed description of the research methodology and copies of the questionnaires, see Appendix A and B.

2 Katharine Hamell, "Women as Bosses," *Fortune,* June 1956, p. 104; Bowman et al, *op. cit.*

3 Respondees in both big businesses and small businesses were personnel directors. Women-in-management respondees were not necessarily personnel directors, but rather were selected only because they were known to hold management positions. Therefore, certain questions were not asked women in management because it was assumed they would not have first-hand information at their disposal to answer the question with validity.

APPENDIX A:

1 As defined by James Lewis, Small Business Administration, Atlanta, Georgia, March 3, 1969: categories broken into three divisions—retail with annual sales less than $1 million, wholesale with annual sales less than $5 million, manufacturing with 250 employees or less. Financial organizations (including banks) are excluded.

116